QUEBEC TRAVEL GUIDE 2023

The Comprehensive Travel Guide to Navigating and Discovering Top Attractions, Activities and Must-see Sights in Quebec

Geneva Walker

CONTENTS

MY QUEBEC VACATION STORY

O nce upon a time, I set off on a magnificent voyage in a distant location. I had no idea what a beautiful and endearing paradise Québec would be. This beautiful province, full of history, culture, and stunning scenery, greeted me with open arms and indelibly inked my trip to Québec in my treasured memory book.

My first steps in La Belle Province took me through the UNESCO World Heritage Site known as Old Québec. This gorgeous residence, which is surrounded by old-defended walls, has cobblestone lanes, charming European architecture, and a wealth of old tales. As I meandered through the seductive lanes, I couldn't help but be drawn in by the delicious aromas of freshly baked crepes and maple treats.

The old buildings in this picturesque city spoke old tales and hinted at dark mysteries. The iconic Château Frontenac was one of these great places, and its royal magnificence helped it to become an exact representation of the Quebecois environment. Its towering spires and turrets soared toward the sky, creating a beautiful silhouette that adorned the horizon.

I instantly feasted my shocked eyes on the vistas, which included the Citadel and the Plains of Abraham. Every moment was a captivating journey, from watching the Changing of the Guard ceremony to lounging in the sun and enjoying live music at the Terrace Dufferin.

As I continued my research of the province, I came across thriving communities that were elegantly interwoven with elements of both French and Canadian culture. As I indulged in delectable meals and sweet delights at neighborhood bistros bordering the banks of the St. Lawrence River, my senses danced with pleasure.

I was mesmerized by the city's nightlife as dusk fell and the metropolis fell under its spell. I experienced an atmosphere of complete enchantment, from seeing outstanding performances at the famous Québec Opera House to taking in the wonder of the famed International Fireworks Competition.

I left the metropolitan attractions and entered the province's pristine regions because nature's beauty drew me. The mystical Montmorency Falls, just a short drive from Québec City, beckoned with its ferocious, flowing beauty. I was mesmerized by Québec's great natural delights, whether I was zip-lining over the thundering falls or wandering along the quaint footbridges.

The Laurentian Mountains, waiting to welcome me, welcomed me with lush valleys and wide stretches painted with vivid colors as I traveled through the beautiful surroundings. Here, I indulged in exhilarating pursuits and quiet periods of introspection while admiring the immense magnificence of towering trees and beautiful lakes.

But with a meeting with powerful aquatic entities, my trip was fully realized. In Tadoussac, I was on a boat admiring majestic humpback and beluga whales, whose elegance and strength were unparalleled against the deep blue backdrop of the sea and sky.

Without recognizing the kindhearted people that make the province so unique, this tale of Québec would fall short. From the busy city streets to the quiet rural charms, the gracious inhabitants' kind smiles, and thoughtful acts stole my heart and ensured that my trip to Québec would become family lore.

And with that, the once-upon-a-time journey ended, leaving me to savor the memories of a world that had mesmerized me. Despite saying goodbye to Québec, this fascinating province with its enthralling scenery, fascinating past, and beloved people will always have a special place in my heart. This was the tale of my trip to Québec, and each chapter was brimming with charm, joy, and awe.

WELCOME TO QUEBEC

Welcome to Quebec! Quebec, located in the center of Canada, is undoubtedly a traveler's paradise. This beautiful region, which has a long history from the 16th century, presents tourists with a distinctive fusion of European elegance with North American energy. You will enter a world of French-Canadian culture, breathtaking architecture, delicious cuisine, and unmatched natural beauty as soon as you step foot on its cobblestoned streets.

Explore and enjoy yourself as you delve into the core of Quebec's history, culture, and natural splendor. Start your journey in Quebec City, the quaint capital of the province. With more than four centuries of history, this UNESCO World Heritage site is a genuine monument to the region's illustrious past. As you walk through the charming Old Quebec's winding alleyways, filled with charming shops and breathtaking cathedrals, you'll be transported back in time. Don't miss the opportunity to see the magnificent Château Frontenac, a well-known site that provides breathtaking views of the St. Lawrence River and the surrounding area.

Beyond the city boundaries, you'll discover that Quebec is bursting with fascinating places to explore. The charming Ile d'Orléans is a must-see and is just a short drive from Quebec City. This picturesque island, which is well-known for its agritourism, makes for the ideal getaway for tasting regional specialties including ice cider, strawberries, and handmade chocolate.

The Charlevoix area is a genuine jewel for thrill-seekers with its untamed terrain and dense woods. There is something for everyone in this magnificent region of Quebec, whether you like guided excursions or are an enthusiastic hiker. The charming villages of Baie-Saint-Paul and La Malbaie are also located in the area, where you can enjoy the famous art scene and regional delicacies.

The biggest city in the province, Montreal, is unquestionably a refuge for culture and globalization. Here, the old-world elegance elegantly fuses with the contemporary urban to create a vibrant metropolis brimming with energy. Immerse yourself in the city's many areas, such as Little Italy, a charming area bursting with real Italian food and espresso cafes, or Plateau Mont-Royal, a bohemian hotspot famed for its colorful buildings and vibrant street art.

Visit the renowned Notre Dame Basilica and enjoy the bustling music and arts scene while strolling through Montreal's lively streets. You will also be treated to various festivals and events, like the famed Montreal Jazz Festival if you can come during the summer.

Mont-Tremblant is a provincial gem that must be noticed. Although Mont-Tremblant is best known for being a winter playground, it also excels in the hot months with various outdoor pursuits, including hiking, mountain biking, and zip-lining. The bustling pedestrian town at the base of the mountain is a year-round attraction for people of all ages thanks to its selection of eating, shopping, and entertainment options.

Overall, Quebec is a place that never ceases to astound and enthrall even the most seasoned tourists. Those who enter this enchanted land are forever changed by its distinctive personality, enthralling history, and magnificent natural beauty. So be ready to say "hello" and "welcome to Quebec," Pack your bags as you set your eyes on this glittering Canadian treasure!

THE FOLLOWING ARE TEN COMPELLING REASONS TO VISIT QUEBEC

If you're considering vacationing in Canada, Quebec should be at the top of your list of places to go. This unique region offers visitors a one-of-a-kind experience by combining European beauty with North American amenities. In this travel guide to Quebec, we'll go over ten intriguing reasons why this province deserves to become your next vacation spot.

First and foremost, Quebec's lovely old-world architecture is a key lure. A UNESCO World Heritage site, Old Quebec City is home to charming 17th-century buildings and has winding cobblestone alleyways. As you tour the historic homes from the 17th and 18th centuries, the cathedrals, and the convents, you'll feel as if you've traveled back in time.

Second, Quebec is a treasure trove of stunning vistas for environment lovers. Numerous pristine national parks, including Parc National de la Gaspésie, Parc National de la Jacques-Cartier, and Parc National des Grands-Jardins, can be found in the region. Each park offers visitors breathtaking views of wooded valleys, raging rivers, and an abundance of animals.

Thirdly, another incentive to visit this French-speaking region is to experience its unique culture. Despite having French as its official language, Quebec is a melting pot of several cultures, creating a thriving and varied creative landscape. Visitors may enjoy delectable food, socialize with welcoming people, and participate in various cultural activities all year, including the Quebec Winter Carnival and the Montreal International Jazz Festival.

Fourth, you'll undoubtedly be inspired by Quebec's vibrant arts scene. The province has a sizable number of performing arts centers, galleries, and museums. For instance, in Montreal, you may treat yourself to a performance at the famed Place des Arts or view modern treasures at the Musée d'art contemporain.

Fifth, Quebec has a wide range of outdoor activities for anyone looking for adventure all year. You may go skiing in Mont Tremblant or try your hand at ice climbing during the winter. Take advantage of the many hiking paths when the weather warms up, go whale watching along the St. Lawrence River, or go on an exhilarating white-water rafting adventure.

Sixth, Quebec offers travelers some of the best French-inspired food in North America. The province's culinary culture is prospering with various gourmet pleasures, from savory poutine to sumptuous sweets. Remember to stop by Montreal's renowned Jean-Talon Market, where you may taste regional foods and handcrafted items.

Quebec's charming tiny towns and villages are the seventh reason to come. Travel through Charlevoix or the Eastern Townships on one of the picturesque roads for a completely immersive experience. These little towns, full of kind residents and breathtaking scenery, are ideal for a peaceful escape from the bustle of the metropolis.

Eighth, many historical sites in Quebec will provide many possibilities for history specialists to learn about Canada's past. Visit the Plains of Abraham, the location of the crucial French-British battle in 1759. Alternately, visit Montreal's Pointe-à-Callière Museum to learn more about the city's extensive archaeological past.

And last, the people of Quebec are renowned for being kind and inviting. Although French is the official language, English is also widely spoken in Quebec. The rich history and tradition of the residents are delighted to be shared, making for a pleasurable and memorable vacation experience for visitors.

Last but not least, Quebec's distinctive festivals and events distinguish it as a must-visit location. Numerous events occur all year round, from the well-known Quebec Winter Carnival to the FestiVoix de Trois-Rivières music festival.

Quebec has plenty to offer everyone, from nature lovers and history enthusiasts to foodies and admirers of the arts. Quebec is unquestionably a popular vacation destination for individuals looking for adventure and leisure because of its rich culture, stunning scenery, various activities, and different events. Plan your trip to Quebec accordingly and make lifelong memories.

INQUIRE ABOUT THESE 15 THINGS BEFORE VISITING QUEBEC.

I t is crucial to be well-prepared when planning your vacation to Quebec, a place rich in history, culture, and scenic beauty, to maximize your enjoyment of your stay. You should be aware of the following fifteen things before visiting Quebec.

French is Quebec's first and predominant official language. Although many people in major cities may be bilingual, knowing some fundamental French phrases is still important. This will make it easier for you to deal with day-to-day issues and demonstrates respect for the local way of life. Travelers are usually liked when they try to interact in the local tongue.

Canadian Dollar (CAD) is the official currency of Quebec. Even if credit cards are frequently used, having cash on hand for minor purchases like transportation or food on the street is a good idea. Cities and large towns have convenient access to banks and ATMs. Also, remember that, like other areas of North America, tipping is expected in Quebec. 15% to 20% is the standard tip on meal bills, and tipping taxi drivers and hotel workers are also customary.

A large metropolis like Montreal and Quebec City, quaint tiny villages like Baie-Saint-Paul, and spectacular natural landmarks like Montmorency Falls are all found in Quebec. Plan a well-balanced schedule that lets you see urban and rural regions to make the most of your trip.

Be ready for a range of weather while going across Quebec. Expect chilly weather and plenty of snowfall if you go during the winter, particularly in ski destinations like Mont Tremblant. On the other hand, summertime may be rather warm and muggy, making it ideal for participating in outdoor activities, festivals, and festivities. Make careful to pack for the season correctly.

Quebecers are proud of their delectable fusion of French and Canadian culinary traditions. Enjoy regional favorites, including poutine, smoked pork sandwiches, and tourtière. Explore the vibrant market scene in Quebec, from the lively Jean-Talon Market in Montreal to the quaint Old Port Market in Quebec City.

Using public transit is a cheap method to get inside large cities. Quebec City has excellent bus services, but Montreal has a well-developed metro system. However, consider hiring a vehicle if you want to go farther-flung locations.

The Winter Carnival in Quebec City and the Jazz Festival in Montreal are just two examples of the many festivals and events that occur all year in Quebec. Schedule your vacation around these occasions to experience the province's thriving culture and entertainment.

Being aware of regional traditions and manners while visiting Quebec is important. Despite their reputation for gracious hospitality, the folks might be more formal in their relationships. When talking to strangers, remain polite and avoid touchy subjects like Quebec's political past.

Quebec is a sanctuary for history buffs because its architecture reflects the province's rich history and culture. Visit the famous Château Frontenac while strolling around the quaint cobblestone alleys of Old Quebec, a UNESCO World Heritage site. Enjoy Montreal's distinctive mix of traditional ambiance and cutting-edge construction.

Quebec has many outdoor recreation opportunities, including

skiing and snowboarding in the Laurentians and whale watching near Tadoussac. Visits to the beautiful Saguenay Fjord and Forillon National Park are highly recommended for nature enthusiasts.

The retail scene in Quebec includes artisanal stores in Quebec City's Petit-Champlain Quarter and hip boutiques in Montreal's Plateau-Mont-Royal district. Visit your local markets to get one-of-a-kind trinkets like maple goods and Inuit paintings.

In terms of lodging, Quebec provides a wide variety of choices. There are accommodations to meet every traveler's requirements and interests, including five-star hotels, quaint bed-and-breakfasts, and affordable hostels.

Any trip should prioritize safety, and traveling through Quebec is no different. It's important to remain alert to your surroundings and apply common sense even though the area is considered relatively safe for visitors. In busy locations, use caution and never leave valuables unattended.

The greatest way to experience Quebec's vibrancy and rich culture is via its thriving cultural scene, which includes theatre, museums, and galleries. Don't miss out on Montreal's Place des Arts, the Musée National des Beaux-Arts du Québec, and the Montreal Museum of Fine Arts.

Spend some time getting to know Quebec's rich culture, which combines Indigenous, French, and British elements. Many interesting experiences await you in Quebec, from the regional cuisine to the province's rich history and culture.

WHAT TO DO IN QUEBEC AND WHAT NOT TO DO

T o make the most of your experience, knowing what to do and what not to do when you plan your trip is crucial. Quebec is a fantastic travel destination because of its distinctive fusion of French and British culture, bustling towns, and breathtaking countryside. As you go through this fascinating area, keep these suggestions in mind.

Steps to Take

1. Embrace the language: With nearly 80% of the people speaking French as their first language, Quebec has a large French-speaking population. Try to get familiar with actual words and phrases like "Bonjour" (good day/hello), "Merci" (thank you), and "Excusez-moi" (excuse me). Your journey will be much more pleasurable since the locals will appreciate your attempts to communicate with them in their language.

2. Experience history firsthand: The province is rich in historical landmarks, including Old Quebec City, which is proud to display its colonial heritage and is a UNESCO World Heritage site. Take a tour with a guide, or take a leisurely walk around the city's charming cobblestone streets.

3. Appreciate food and culture: The delectable cuisine of Quebec is well-known for being a fusion of French and Canadian elements. Don't be afraid to indulge in traditional foods like tarte au sucre, tourtière, and poutine. To learn more about Quebec's vibrant culture, go to cultural events like the Montreal Jazz Festival, Quebec City's Winter Carnival, or nearby comedy acts.

4. Take advantage of nature: Quebec is proud of its stunning landscapes, from the imposing cliffs of the Gaspé Peninsula to the tranquil woods of Mont-Tremblant Provincial Park. A trek, a whale-watching excursion, or a scenic trip on the Le Massif de Charlevoix Railway are all recommended. Take advantage of your sense of adventure and discover Quebec's outdoors.

What To Avoid

1. Don't skip on the less well-known locations: While Montreal and Quebec City are common stops on most itineraries, smaller towns like Sherbrooke, Saguenay, and Île d'Orléans have hidden beauties and a feel for genuine life in Quebec. To fully appreciate the province's uniqueness, take the time to explore these lesser-known locations.

2. Contrasts should be avoided since Quebec's French-Canadian culture is distinct and should not be compared directly to French culture. Recognize the distinctions and appreciate the distinctiveness of Quebecois culture despite the similarities.

3. Tipping is common in Quebec, although it's important not to go overboard. In general, 15% is the right amount to tip for most services, but 20% should be saved for great service.

4. Never underestimate Quebec's weather; it may be anything from hot and muggy in the summer to chilly and snowy in the winter. Always dress for the season and be ready for abrupt temperature changes.

5. Avoid contentious subjects: Respecting people's beliefs and views is important wherever you go. Avoid bringing up sensitive subjects like Quebec's sovereignty or language issues since doing so might result in tense arguments and awkward situations.

By adhering to these recommendations, you'll be prepared to

explore Quebec City's charming streets, immerse yourself in Montreal's dynamic cultural scene, and learn about the province's immense natural beauty. Take pleasure in your trip and take in everything Quebec offers.

QUEBEC VISA REQUIREMENTS

Q uebec, the biggest province in Canada, is home to a captivating combination of energetic cities, spectacular natural beauty, a thriving arts and cultural scene, and an intriguing past. Organizing your visa needs is the first step to a wonderful vacation if you're considering a trip to this unusual location. The many visa categories, eligibility requirements, application procedures, and important advice are all broken down in this guide to assist you in getting to Quebec.

Quebec Visitor Visas

Canada governs Quebec and abides by its rules on visas. Before visiting Quebec, travelers from most nations must get a Temporary Resident Visa (TRV) or an Electronic Travel Authorization (eTA).

Temporary Resident Visa (TRV): If you are from a nation where a visa is necessary to enter Canada, you must apply for a TRV. You can remain in Canada for a brief term, often at least six months. You may apply for a TRV as a Single Entry or Multiple Entry visa, depending on your travel requirements.

You must get an electronic travel authorization (eTA) if you are flying to Quebec from a nation where visas are not required. An eTA is a digital document associated with your passport number valid for five years or until your Passport expires, whichever comes first.

With a few exceptions, US nationals need to have a current passport with them when they visit Quebec and are free from the eTA and TRV requirements.

Application Method

Visit the official immigration website of the Canadian government at www.canada.ca to start your visa application. Once there, do the following:

1. Assess your eligibility to see whether you need an eTA or a TRV for your trip to Quebec by completing the online questionnaire.

2. Create an account: If required, create an account on the online application site for the Government of Canada.

3. Compile supporting papers, such as trip itineraries, passport copies, and evidence of financial assistance.

4. Complete your application by providing the correct information on the online form and submitting it with the required paperwork.

5. Pay the required fees: The application cost for a TRV is $100, and the application price for an eTA is $7. These costs must be paid online using a legitimate credit card.

6. Biometrics: Some candidates may be required to submit their biometrics (fingerprints and photos) at a legitimate visa application facility for an extra fee of CAD 85.

7. Check the status of your application by logging into your account to follow the development of your application and reply to any follow-up inquiries from the visa office.

8. If your application is approved, you will get your passport TRV sticker and eTA confirmation.

Advice for Quebec visa seekers

- Submit your application as soon as possible. Processing duration for visas might vary from a few days (for an eTA) to several weeks (for a TRV).

Your Passport must be valid for at least six months after the day you want to enter Quebec.

- Health insurance: Get comprehensive travel and health insurance for your trip since the cost of medical treatment in Quebec might be high and because the Canadian government can ask you for evidence of coverage.

- Invitation letter: If you are traveling to Quebec to visit friends or family, a letter of invitation from your hosts attesting to your connection with them and the reason for your trip might help your application.

- Intended purpose: Clearly state your visit's objective (tourist, business, or research) and back it up with appropriate evidence.

- Documents demonstrating your family, work, or property-related links should be included to prove your wish to return to your native country.

You'll be well on your way to experiencing Quebec's allure and navigating the visa application procedure with confidence and simplicity if you keep informed about the visa requirements for Quebec and adhere to the instructions outlined in this guide.

IS A VISA REQUIRED TO ENTER QUEBEC?

U nderstanding the visa requirements is a crucial aspect of your preparations if you want to visit Quebec, a bustling and culturally diverse province in eastern Canada. Despite having a distinctively francophone character, Quebec is a part of Canada. Therefore observing the rules regarding visas is quite important. This manual will assist you in navigating the procedure, concentrating on the Quebec-specific visa guidelines and specifications.

To start, your country, the purpose of your trip, and the time you want to stay will determine whether or not you require a visa to enter Quebec. It's important to remember that whether they are American citizens or possess a valid Canadian visa, visa-exempt tourists must still get an Electronic Travel Authorization (eTA) before entering Quebec via an airport.

Who May Go To Quebec Without A Visa?

Visitors visiting Quebec for vacation, business, or family trips lasting less than six months are not required to have a visa if they are from a nation exempt from Canada's visa requirements. These nations include the United States, every nation that is a part of the European Union, Australia, Japan, and others. An eTA, which may be purchased online with a valid passport, a credit card, and an email account, is required for visa-exempt nationals to travel to Quebec. The application procedure is simple, and your eTA is often approved in minutes or hours. It is valid for up to five years or until the expiration of your Passport.

Who Needs A Visa To Visit Quebec?

You will need a Temporary Resident Visa (TRV) to enter Quebec if you are a citizen of a nation that is not excluded from visa requirements for Canada. Start by going to the Government of Canada website and following their instructions for submitting an online form or a paper application, presenting supporting paperwork, and paying a fee to apply for a TRV. It is important to apply well before your intended departure since the processing period for your TRV application may vary based on your country of residency.

What Qualifications Are Needed For Employment, Study, Or Immigration Visas?

There are many visa procedures, whether you want to work, study, or immigrate to Quebec. Start by visiting the websites of the Quebec government and Citizenship and Immigration Canada for comprehensive instructions and application forms for employment and study permits. The website of the Ministry of Immigration, Francisation, and Integration provides more information for people looking to immigrate to Quebec.

Remember that owing to the current COVID-19 epidemic, quarantines may be necessary for both visa-exempt and visa-required passengers. Thus it is strongly advised to remain up to speed with the most recent information from the Canadian government.

Depending on several variables, such as your nationality, the purpose of your travel, and the length of your stay, you may or may not require a visa to visit Quebec. For air travel, nationals of nations without visa requirements need an eTA, while those from nations with visa requirements need a TRV. Before beginning your trip to Quebec, the French-speaking jewel of Canada, consider your unique circumstances and check the essential government websites for accurate and up-to-date information.

LIST OF COUNTRIES WHOSE CITIZENS DO NOT NEED VISAS

W e thoroughly review the countries whose residents are not needed to get a visa to visit Quebec to aid you in this procedure. Keep in mind that as Quebec is a part of Canada, the national visa legislation also applies to the province.

To start with, you're lucky if you're an American citizen! Quebec and the rest of Canada do not need a visa for entry. The only requirements are a current passport and, sometimes, an Electronic Travel Authorization (eTA).

Travel to Quebec and the whole of Canada is visa-free for nationals of the European Union, Iceland, Norway, and Switzerland. These tourists' travel procedure is made easier by needing an eTA before leaving.

There is a sizable list of nations that are also free from visa requirements in addition to this. These countries, to mention a few, include Australia, New Zealand, Japan, and South Korea, whose people may go to Quebec without having to go through the troublesome visa application procedure. Please be aware that visitors from these nations must also apply for an eTA before their trip.

To clarify, residents of a few Latin American nations, including Chile, Brazil, and Mexico, are also excluded from the necessity for a visa. If they have an eTA in advance, they may easily tour Quebec's beautiful landscapes and diverse culture.

It's crucial to remember that different entrance criteria may apply for any trip to Quebec, regardless of whether you qualify for a visa exemption. These requirements depend on the purpose of your trip and how long you want to remain. The most precise and current information may be found by visiting the Government of Canada's official website.

Even if visitors from various nations may visit Quebec without a visa, getting an eTA is still necessary for hassle-free travel. Make sure to plan your trip well in advance, considering your unique travel needs and necessary paperwork, so that you may enjoy Quebec's enchantment without any problems. Travel safely!

THE FOLLOWING COUNTRIES DON'T NEED VISAS FOR THEIR CITIZENS.

You will have greater freedom while arranging your vacation to Quebec if you are a citizen of one of a few designated nations. In this enlightening guide, we'll provide important information on visa-free travel regulations for certain nations to help you prepare for your trip to Quebec.

Quebec is one of Canada's most cosmopolitan and diversified provinces; as such, it draws a sizable number of visitors each year. Canada has established visa-exemption procedures for travelers from different nations to help make travel easier. Passport holders from countries under these regulations can visit Quebec and the rest of Canada without obtaining a visa.

As a result of political agreements between Canada and various countries, the list of nations whose citizens are not required to get a visa often changes. But many nations now make use of these advantages.

For instance, visa applications are unnecessary for travelers from the United States, the United Kingdom, Australia, and many European nations. Thanks to this exception, they are free to enjoy Quebec's natural beauty, its rich culture, and its welcoming people.

It's crucial to remember that even though citizens of these nations do not need a visa, they must still get an Electronic Travel Authorization (eTA) before traveling to Quebec by plane. This quick online procedure guarantees a smooth journey for qualified passengers since it only requires them to respond to a few required questions that aid the Canadian authorities in determining any possible dangers.

Other nations in Asia, South America, and the Caribbean benefit from the visa-free policy in addition to the United States, the United Kingdom, Australia, and most of Europe. For instance, citizens of Japan, New Zealand, Israel, and South Korea don't need a visa to enjoy Quebec's expansive natural beauty, famous buildings, and distinctive gastronomic offerings.

Last, it's important to remember that visa-free travel is often restricted to brief stays, such as vacations or business meetings. Longer visits to Quebec, such as those made for work or school, may require extra visas or permits.

It is no longer necessary for citizens of other nations to get a visa to visit Quebec. This benefit makes traveling easier and allows tourists from certain countries to concentrate on creating amazing experiences while seeing the province's unmatched attractiveness and charm. Always double-check with the official Canadian government website or consulate for the most recent information since visa rules are subject to change over time. We wish you an amazing journey across Quebec's stunning scenery and vibrant towns!

NATIONS FOR WHICH QUEBEC REQUIRES A VISA

Do you need an airport transit visa to go to Quebec for business or pleasure? No more worries! You may learn all about airport transit visas in Quebec from our helpful guide.

Understanding Quebec Airport Transit Visas

Let's first define an airport transit visa. An airport transit visa allows you to travel through an airport's international area without entering the host nation, in this example, Canada. Quebec is a province of Canada and is subject to the same visa procedures as the rest of the nation should not be overlooked.

To be clear, you could need an airport transit visa if you're flying into a Canadian airport but don't plan to leave or go through immigration. Although you cannot enter Canada with this visa, you may change planes in the airport's transit area.

Who Needs A Transit Visa For An Airport?

An airport transit visa is unnecessary for everyone passing through a Canadian airport en route. Citizens of a few nations are free from the need for an airport transit visa. The United States, as well as other nations, are among these nations. On the website of the Canadian government is a comprehensive list of nations whose residents do not need an airport transit visa.

However, you may need an airport transit visa if you are a citizen of a nation that needs a visa to enter Canada and will pass through a Canadian airport.

How Can I Get A Transit Visa For An Airport?

Your home country's Canadian embassy or consulate may help you apply for an airport transit visa. The procedure is quick and simple to understand, making it a stress-free experience. What you'll need for your application is the following:

1. a Temporary Resident Visa application form (IMM 5257) has been completed.
2. Two current photos the size of a passport that includes your name and birthdate on the reverse.
3. a current passport without the final page that has at least one blank page.
4. A confirmed airline ticket is proof of your intended next destination.
5. a letter from your work and, if appropriate, a letter of invitation from the Canadian host.
6. payment for the processing fee, if necessary.

Please be aware that extra paperwork could be needed based on your citizenship and trip itinerary.

Applying for your transit visa well before your intended trip dates is advised. Processing timeframes range from a few days to weeks for most nations. Additionally, you should regularly check the Canadian government's website for updates on your nation's particular visa requirements.

Should I Rather Submit A Visitor Visa Application?

A visiting visa may be more appropriate if you want to leave the airport and tour Quebec or Canada, even if it's just for a brief stopover. An airport transit visa is only required inside the approved international transit area. Depending on your nationality, you can also request an Electronic Travel Authorization (eTA) for a brief visit to Canada.

If you follow the instructions and prerequisites in this guide, acquiring an airport transit visa for Quebec is a simple procedure. To guarantee a smooth passage through Quebec's airports, be aware and organize your journey appropriately.

TRANSIT VISA FOR AIRPORTS

D o you need an airport transit visa to go to Quebec for business or pleasure? No more worries! You may learn all about airport transit visas in Quebec from our helpful guide.

Understanding Quebec Airport Transit Visas

Let's first define an airport transit visa. An airport transit visa allows you to travel through an airport's international area without entering the host nation, in this example, Canada. Quebec is a province of Canada and is subject to the same visa procedures as the rest of the nation should not be overlooked.

To be clear, you could need an airport transit visa if you're flying into a Canadian airport but don't plan to leave or go through immigration. Although you cannot enter Canada with this visa, you may change planes in the airport's transit area.

Who Needs A Transit Visa For An Airport?

An airport transit visa is unnecessary for everyone passing

through a Canadian airport en route. Citizens of a few nations are free from needing an airport transit visa. The United States, as well as other nations, are among these nations. On the website of the Canadian government is a comprehensive list of nations whose residents do not need an airport transit visa.

However, you may need an airport transit visa if you are a citizen of a nation that needs a visa to enter Canada and will pass through a Canadian airport.

How Can I Get A Transit Visa For An Airport?

Your home country's Canadian embassy or consulate may help you apply for an airport transit visa. The procedure is quick and simple to understand, making it a stress-free experience. What you'll need for your application is the following:

1. a Temporary Resident Visa application form (IMM 5257) has been completed.
2. Two current photos the size of a passport that includes your name and birthdate on the reverse.
3. a current passport without the final page that has at least one blank page.
4. A confirmed airline ticket is proof of your intended next destination.
5. a letter from your work and, if appropriate, a letter of invitation from the Canadian host.
6. payment for the processing fee, if necessary.

Please know that extra paperwork could be needed based on your citizenship and trip itinerary.

Applying for your transit visa well before your intended trip dates is advised. Processing timeframes range from a few days to a few weeks for the majority of nations. Additionally, you should regularly check the Canadian government's website for updates on your nation's particular visa requirements.

Should I Rather Submit A Visitor Visa Application?

A visiting visa may be more appropriate if you want to leave the airport and tour Quebec or Canada, even if it's just for a brief stopover. An airport transit visa is only required inside the approved international transit area. Depending on your nationality, you can also request an Electronic Travel Authorization (eTA) for a brief visit to Canada.

In conclusion, if you follow the instructions and prerequisites in this guide, acquiring an airport transit visa for Quebec is a simple procedure. To guarantee a smooth passage through Quebec's airports, be aware and organize your journey appropriately.

REQUIRED DOCUMENTS

K nowing the necessary paperwork for a smooth travel experience is crucial when planning vacations to Quebec's lovely and culturally rich province. We'll go into great depth about the paperwork you'll need in our travel guide so you may enjoy your time in Quebec to the fullest.

First, your Passport is the most important document you will need wherever you are going. Your Passport, which acts as your main form of identity while you are in Canada, must be current. Some nations need that their passports remain valid for at least six months beyond the anticipated departure date from Canada. It is strongly advised to have a physical photocopy and a scanned copy of your Passport's information page in case it is lost or stolen. Secondly, you could require a visiting visa or an Electronic Travel Authorization (eTA) to enter Canada, depending on your nationality and the purpose of your trip. Check the official website of the Canadian government or contact the Canadian embassy or consulate in your country to find out whether you qualify. If a visa or eTA is necessary for your trip, apply well before your departure to prevent unforeseen delays. Although getting an eTA is often as straightforward as submitting an online application and paying a nominal cost, obtaining a visa may need extra paperwork, expenses, and processing time.

You will need a work visa if you travel to Quebec on business or want to work there temporarily. You must provide a work offer letter from a Canadian company, pertinent papers demonstrating your credentials, and any other documentation the Canadian government may want to achieve this. To guarantee a smooth application procedure, it's crucial to carefully study and adhere to the government of Canada's guidelines.

You'll likely require a study permit to attend school in Quebec. You must provide the following:

- Evidence of acceptance from an authorized Canadian educational institution.
- Proof of financial assistance.
- Proof of identification to get a study permit.

Prior to requesting a study permit, foreign students need additionally get a Quebec Acceptance Certificate (CAQ) from the Ministère de l'Immigration, de la Francisation et de l'Intégration (MIFI).

The main language in Quebec is French. Thus having a working knowledge of it is helpful. Consider having a little French phrasebook if you need to speak French better. Even though English is widely used in tourist destinations, being able to speak French will make your trip more pleasurable as you discover Quebec's rich francophone culture.

Another crucial document for your trip to Quebec is travel insurance. Make sure you have a current travel insurance plan that offers coverage for, among other things, medical costs, trip cancellation, and lost baggage. In the case of an accident or sickness, having this paper on hand and understanding how to access and utilize your insurance provider's services may help you save a lot of stress.

Lastly, always maintain digital copies of your important papers in a safe location. Where feasible, have a physical copy as a backup to ensure trouble-free travel. This includes your travel insurance policy, employment or study permit, Passport, visa, or electronic travel authorization.

Before beginning your travel to the picturesque province of

Quebec, ensuring all the required documentation is in order is crucial. You are prepared to explore and revel in the vivid sights, tastes, and experiences Quebec has to offer now that you are armed with these papers and a spirit of adventure.

TIME REQUIRED
TO GET A VISA

Are you going to scenic Quebec to explore its fascinating cultural heritage? There is something for every tourist in this lovely province, whether you want to wander through the cobblestone alleys of Old Quebec, trek Mont Tremblant, or discover Montreal's busy downtown. It's important to comprehend the procedure and time required to get a visa before deciding on your schedule to ensure a hassle-free journey.

How to Determine Your Visa Requirements:

First and foremost, you must ascertain if a visa is required for entry into Quebec. While foreign visitors can need a visa depending on their nationality, Canadian citizens and permanent residents are exempt from this rule. Only an Electronic Travel Authorization (eTA) is required for visa-exempt nationalities to enter Quebec for brief visits. To determine whether you qualify for a visa exemption, visit the Government of Canada's website.

A Temporary Resident Visa (TRV) application:

If a visa is necessary for you to enter Quebec, you should likely apply for a Temporary Resident Visa (TRV). You are granted temporary entry into Canada using this document for travel, temporary employment, or visits with relatives. A TRV application must be submitted before traveling to Quebec.

Processing Time for Your Visa Application:

The time it takes to process a visa application for travel to Quebec varies greatly depending on your nationality, the visa office handling your application, and the quality and completeness of your supporting documentation. The processing of your application by the Canadian authorities takes 2 to 6 weeks on average.

However, it's important to note that processing times could be lengthier during busy travel periods or when applications surge. It is highly encouraged to begin the visa application procedure before your anticipated departure date to prevent last-minute problems.

How to Quicken the Visa Process:

The following advice may help you apply for a visa to go to Quebec more quickly and easily:

1. Start by reading up on the visa criteria and application procedure on the website of the Canadian government. For an application to be successful, the information must be accurate and current.

2. you prevent delays brought on by mistakes, be sure you fill out your visa application form fully and precisely.

3. assemble all required supporting documentation, including a passport-sized picture, financial verification, and a trip schedule. Ensure that these papers adhere to the visa office's criteria for format and content.

4. Pay the necessary procedural costs to get your visa. Your application can be delayed or rejected due to incomplete or inaccurate payments.

5. Apply well in advance of the date you want to go. As was already said, processing timelines might vary greatly, so applying early gives you a cushion in case of delays.

One of the most important parts of organizing your trip to Quebec is getting your visa as soon as possible. When planning your vacation, keep in mind the necessary prerequisites and processing timeframes. Using the advice in this manual, you can ensure that your visa application goes smoothly, freeing you to look forward to a wonderful vacation in Quebec's warm embrace.

THE COMPREHENSIVE ONE-WEEK ITINERARY TO SEVEN DAYS IN QUEBEC

During a seven-day getaway to Quebec, Canada's French-speaking province, immerse yourself in the region's culture, history, and natural beauty. Any travel enthusiast who likes variety in their terrain, friendly folks, and world-class attractions should visit Quebec. There is something for everyone, with charming towns, thriving cities, and stunning national parks. This comprehensive one-week guide to Quebec includes a day-by-day plan to pique your interest in new experiences, sate your appetite, and make you feel like a part of la belle province.

Day 1: Montreal
Get a taste of Euro-American charm when you arrive in Montreal, the cultural center of Quebec and the second-largest French-speaking metropolis in the world. Explore 2Old Montreal's cobblestone streets in the morning and stop at the magnificent Notre Dame Basilica. Then, savor some Quebecois fare at a neighborhood cafe. Remember to eat poutine, which is Montreal's

national dish. Spend the day exploring the Plateau Mont-Royal, a hip neighborhood famed for its brightly painted homes and paintings, and then go to Mount Royal Park for sweeping views of the city skyline.

Day 2: Quebec City to Montreal

Enjoy a morning visit to Montreal's renowned Jean-Talon Market before you depart for a sample of fresh local cuisine and handcrafted goods. Then, start your 2.5-hour trip to Quebec City, one of North America's oldest and most charming towns, along the picturesque St. Lawrence River. Once there, stroll casually around Old Quebec's defensive walls, a UNESCO World Heritage site brimming with historical significance and beautiful architecture. Explore Quartier Petit Champlain's artisan stores and cafés, stroll along the lovely Terrasse Dufferin, and conclude the day with a delectable lunch at a French-style eatery.

Day 3: Quebec City

Visit Montmorency Falls, a magnificent waterfall with breathtaking views and paths, to start your day. Visit the Plains of Abraham in the afternoon; it's a historic battleground with beautiful outdoor space and enlightening displays. Spend the evening visiting Old Quebec, taking in the quaint alleyways and lit structures like the Chateau Frontenac.

Day 4: Charlevoix to Quebec City

From Quebec City, go east to Charlevoix, a charming area renowned for its beautiful natural surroundings and cultural legacy. The hamlet of Baie-Saint-Paul, with its thriving art galleries, distinctive shops, and wonderful restaurants, should be your first visit. You may explore the park's various hiking routes and take in breathtaking views by traveling a short distance to Parc National des Grands-Jardins.

Day 5: Tadoussac whale watching

On the fifth day, take a day excursion to Tadoussac, a seaside town. Tadoussac is situated at the stunning confluence of the Saguenay and St. Lawrence Rivers. Tadoussac, well-known for having a wealth of marine life, is the ideal location for a whale-watching tour. You may witness various whale species between May and

October, including the fascinating beluga. A seafood feast at one of Tadoussac's quaint riverbank eateries will round off your day.

Day 6: Investigate the Fjord du Saguenay

Visit Fjord-du-Saguenay National Park for a journey through some of Quebec's most magnificent natural settings. This enormous protected region is renowned for its stunning cliffs created by glaciers, thick woods, and abundant animals. The fjord's unmatched splendor will leave you speechless whether you kayak across the lit waters or trek along one of the park's gorgeous pathways.

Day 7: Arrival back in Montreal and departure

As you return to Montreal for your trip, bid Quebec goodbye. Take a side trip to Trois-Rivières, a historic city where the Saint-Maurice and St. Lawrence rivers converge. Before returning to Montreal to round off your memorable trip to Quebec, take an interesting tour of the city's Old Prison and dine at a riverfront restaurant.

This seven-day tour highlights Quebec's distinctiveness and charm while providing a fusion of history, culture, and natural beauty. Your one-week trip to Quebec will leave you with lifelong memories, from the energetic streets of Montreal to the beautiful landscapes of Charlevoix and the whales of Tadoussac.

TRAVELING IN QUEBEC

E xploring Quebec, a province in eastern Canada with a largely French-speaking population, might be exciting. Quebec is the biggest Canadian province by land size and provides a wide variety of attractions, cultures, and landscapes that will astonish any visitor. Knowing the various transit options and insider tips for navigating Quebec can help you make the most of your vacation to "La Belle province."

Travel By Air

Air travel may be the quickest and most practical choice for people who want to traverse Quebec's extensive terrain. Flying is an effective means to travel further distances within the province due to the abundance of airports in large cities like Montreal and Quebec City and smaller airports in areas like Saguenay and Gaspésie. Air Canada is the main airline that flies into and out of Quebec. However, Porter Airlines and WestJet also operate flights there.

Travel By Train

For those who prefer a leisurely pace, traveling across Quebec by train is a picturesque and pleasurable option. The primary railway company, VIA Rail, offers a smooth and effective service linking significant cities, including Montreal, Quebec City, and Ottawa. In addition, the train stops in a few smaller towns, making it simpler to reach picturesque and less traveled areas.

Travel By Bus

Intercity bus travel in Quebec is an economical and dependable choice for tourists on a tight budget. Numerous services are offered both inside the province and outside of it by bus companies such as Greyhound, Orleans Express, and Intercar. Modern, air-conditioned buses in Quebec often provide Wi-Fi, enabling you to remain connected while traveling.

Renting A Car And Driving

Renting a vehicle is a great option if you want to go outside of major cities or explore Quebec at your own leisure. However, before starting an extended road journey throughout the province, remember that most road signs are in French and that driving customs may vary from your own. Make sure to acquaint yourself with Quebec's driving regulations and get ready to adjust to any peculiarities, such as Montreal's ban on right turns at red lights.

Using Public Transit

The largest cities in Quebec have dependable and effective public transportation systems. With its large metro and bus networks, Montreal has one of the greatest networks in North America. With a fleet of buses, the local public transportation company RTC serves the city and its surrounding areas in Quebec City. At the same time, the Ecolobus transports visitors through the famed Old Quebec neighborhood. A cheap and environmentally responsible method to go about cities and experience local culture is by using public transportation.

Biking

Quebec is a cycling lover's heaven for people who like an athletic trip. La Route Verte, the province's network of linked bicycle paths, spans more than 5,000 kilometers. For visitors looking to explore on two wheels, major cities include rental shops and bike-sharing schemes like Montreal's BIXI system. Cycling enthusiasts will love Quebec's generally level landscape and designated bike lanes, which make it a terrific vacation spot.

After familiarizing yourself with the various modes of transportation and being able to choose the one that best meets your travel needs, tastes, and financial situation, moving about Quebec is a snap. Regardless of the method you choose, a visit to this alluring Canadian province ensures an outstanding experience that will have you wanting to come back time and time again.

A GUIDE TO PUBLIC TRANSIT

I ts comprehensive and effective public transit system makes exploring the dynamic province of Quebec simple. This guide will help you find your way around the different public transit alternatives accessible to you, whether you're riding across Mont-Tremblant, navigating the cobblestone streets of Old Quebec, or going to the outermost corners of the province.

Transportation In Cities: Transit Services

Transportation in Quebec refers to traveling effectively and sustainably. Two significant cities in the province, Montreal and Quebec City, each have a unique public transportation system.

It is simple to get about the city because of the extensive bus and subway network that Montreal's Société de Transport de Montréal (STM) runs. The STM serves a sizable portion of Montreal and its environs with four metro lines and more than 200 bus routes. The prices are affordable, with single-ride and monthly passes available, as well as senior and student discounts.

Traveling between the city's many neighborhoods is simple, thanks to the large bus service provided by Quebec City's Réseau de Transport de la Capitale (RTC). In addition to ordinary buses, RTC operates an eco-friendly shuttle service called Ecolobus that travels through the center of Old Quebec during the summer months.

Both cities now provide paratransit services for those with limited mobility, guaranteeing an inclusive public transportation experience.

Cycling Is A Popular Choice

In Quebec, biking is a well-liked mode of transportation since it is a healthy and ecologically beneficial alternative to driving. The bike-sharing schemes in Montreal and Quebec City, BIXI in Montreal, and RTC's Vélo in Quebec City are quite well-developed. With docking stations dispersed across cities, these programs provide a practical and affordable way to see the city on two wheels.

Services For Commuter Trains

Individuals who go to suburban or remote locations often utilize commuter rail services, but most individuals who travel inside metropolitan areas depend on buses or metro lines. Six suburban rail lines are run by Montreal's Réseau de transport métropolitain (RTM). Once operational, Quebec City's projected Réseau Express de la Capitale (REC) would provide a quick and easy means to go from the city center to the suburbs.

Buses And Trains For Intercity Travel

Due to the size of Quebec's area, intercity travel is frequent among residents and visitors. The province is served by bus companies linking larger cities and smaller settlements. Companies like Orléans Express, Intercar, and Limocar provide speedy and pleasant transportation between locations, with ticket costs ranging according to amenities and trip distance.

For those who prefer using the train, VIA Rail Canada serves several cities and villages around Quebec. Many transport options exist, from vintage rail trips to cutting-edge high-speed service between Montreal and Quebec City.

Looking Into Rural Quebec

Rural Quebec depends on smaller bus companies and local transportation services, while cities and bigger towns have well-developed public transit networks. Numerous companies, including Autobus Maheux and Transport Adapted et Collectif des Collines, provide transportation to local locations with scheduled timetables or on-demand reservations.

This public transportation guide should make it easy for you to navigate Quebec, whether taking a bus to see the historical sights in Quebec City or bicycling along the Lachine Canal in Montreal. By choosing environmentally friendly modes of transportation, you'll be helping the environment and fully experiencing La Belle Province's distinctive beauty.

HOW TO NAVIGATE QUEBEC

Q uebec, the second-most populated province in Canada, is rich in culture, history, and magnificent natural beauty. This largely French-speaking territory extends from the Atlantic coast to the Great Lakes and Hudson Bay. Planning your transportation choices is essential for a smooth and pleasurable trip, whether traveling to Montreal's modern city or Charlevoix's charming villages. In this book, you'll find helpful pointers and suggestions on moving about Quebec with ease and flair.

Using Public Transit

Travelers in Quebec have several alternatives for getting about, both inside the cities and between the various areas. While visiting Montreal and Quebec City, you can count on their public transportation systems to be effective and user-friendly. In Montreal and Quebec City, respectively, the Société de Transport de Montréal (STM) and Réseau de Transport de la Capitale (RTC) provide complete bus and metro services. Consider getting a tourist card if you plan on staying in the city for a few days so you may take unlimited rides for a certain amount of time.

Travel By Train

Train travel is among the most elegant and practical methods of getting between the main cities of Quebec. Quebec City and Montreal are connected by VIA Train Canada, the nation's national train service, which provides daily departures at different times. You may enjoy the province's breathtaking scenery along the St. Lawrence River during the two-and-a-half-hour drive between these cities. In addition, VIA Rail offers links to Charlevoix, the Gaspé Peninsula, and the Laurentians, making it possible for you to travel to most of Quebec's well-known locations.

Carpooling And Rental Vehicles

The best flexibility for seeing the province at your leisure is provided by renting a vehicle. Significant rental firms exist in Quebec's major cities and airports, including Hertz, Avis, and Enterprise. Booking in advance is suggested since renting a vehicle may be pricey, particularly during the busy season. Alternatively, you may carpool with other passengers to the same location using services like Amigo Express or BlaBlaCar.

Biking And Sharing Bikes

Famous cities in Quebec are becoming increasingly bicycle-friendly, with many bike lanes and designated riding routes. Renting a bike is a great way to see Montreal, Quebec City, and other pedestrian-friendly regions like Île d'Orléans. Bike rental establishments may be found in several popular tourist destinations. Additionally, you can easily pick up and drop off a bike while exploring, thanks to Montreal's BIXI bike-sharing system, which has over 5,000 bikes available at 700 stations.

Ridesharing And Cabs

In Quebec's largest cities, taxis are commonly accessible and may be hailed on the street or reserved in advance via regional taxi firms like Taxi Coop or Taxi Diamond. Uber and Lyft are great choices for tourists who like ridesharing since they are available in Montreal and Quebec City. However, keep in mind that prices might increase during busy times and peak hours.

Distance-Traveling Buses

Long-distance routes connecting Quebec's villages and cities are serviced at affordable rates by coach buses like Orléans Express and Intercar. Depending on your location, buses may provide lower prices and more frequent departures than trains. Purchasing tickets online is advised to reserve a seat and take advantage of any discounts.

Ultimately, all kinds of tourists may easily get about in Quebec. This lovely region is yours to explore, whether you decide to stay with public transportation or hire a vehicle for the ultimate road trip. So grab your luggage and prepare to be completely enthralled by Quebec's lively culture, attractive architecture, and stunning scenery.

HOW TO NAVIGATE THE QUEBEC METRO

It is quick and easy to get about the busy metropolis via the Quebec metro system, often referred to as the Montreal Metro. This comprehensive manual offers advice on everything from buying tickets to navigating the different stations to help you get the most out of your Metro experience.

Before Starting:

Learn the structure of the city's public transportation system, which comprises four separate lines: Green, Orange, Yellow, and Blue, before you start your Quebec Metro experience. Each route includes many stations and links to the airport, downtown Montreal, and tourist destinations. Online or at Metro stations, a map of the network is available.

Getting Tickets:

You'll need a valid ticket or transport pass to use the Quebec Metro. A variety of fare alternatives are offered to meet your travel requirements:
- Single Trip Tickets: These are available at all Metro stations' automated ticket booths and are good for only one trip. They're

your best choice if you want to use the Metro sometimes while traveling.

- Day Passes A day ticket allows unrestricted travel for 24 hours, which is a better choice if you want to use the Metro more often while in town.

- 3-day, Weekly, or Monthly Passes: If you want to remain in Quebec longer, you may choose a ticket that entitles you to unrestricted travel for three days, a week, or a month.

- OPUS Card: Frequent visitors to Quebec may find it advantageous to buy an OPUS card, which can be filled with individual trips or tickets and facilitates smooth transit on public transportation, including buses and trains.

Utilizing The Metro

You may utilize the Metro after you have your ticket or transit pass. Here are some pointers to make your vacation go smoothly:

1. Validate your ticket before boarding the Metro if you're using a single-ride ticket. The validity of passes and OPUS cards are not required.

2. Timing: Try to travel outside rush hour, often between 9 am and 4 pm or after 7 pm on weekdays. Weekends often need more activity.

3. Transfers: If your route calls for them, be prepared to change lines. Follow the instructions while changing lines, and don't hesitate to approach the personnel for help if you need it.

4. Reading Maps: Become familiar with the Metro map to help you identify the proper transfers and effectively plan your itinerary. Every Metro vehicle and stop has a map.

5. Watch out for departure signs, or "Sorties," as they are called in French. Follow these signs to the closest street to continue your journey to Quebec.

6. Accessibility: The Quebec Metro has elevators and ramps at most of its stations to benefit those who are less mobile. To locate a list of stations that are accessible, search online.

7. Etiquette: Remember to adhere to fundamental transportation

etiquette, including allowing people to join the Metro car before they depart, not obstructing doors or aisles, and minimizing noise levels.

Security And Safety:

Although the Quebec Metro is a reputable and secure method of transportation, it's important to stay alert and take the usual safety measures. Avoid distractions, keep your possessions safe, and consider your surroundings when riding the Metro. Each station has a security call box and surveillance cameras in case of emergency.

The best way for tourists to see what Quebec offers is by using the metro system to explore the city. Quebec's distinctive art, culture, and history may be experienced within a few Metro stations thanks to the well-maintained network of trains and buses. We hope this guide gives you all the knowledge you want for a smooth trip via the Montreal Metro. Enjoy your journey!

UTILIZING A TRAM

Greetings and welcome to your thorough "How to Use a Tram" tutorial in Quebec. Trams are now a practical, cutting-edge, and environmentally responsible method to see Quebec's famous tourist destinations. We'll provide you with all the pertinent, current information you need about the tram system in this guide so you can confidently get about and enjoy your time in this beautiful city.

Getting Tickets:

To ride the tram, you'll first need to purchase a ticket. Single-use tickets, day passes, and monthly passes are just a few available ticket choices. Tickets may be bought online or through machines positioned at different tram stops. Remember to use the platform ticket-validation devices to scan your ticket before boarding.

Become acquainted with the map:

It will be much simpler to navigate Quebec if you spend a few minutes looking through the tram network map. You can effortlessly plan your journey thanks to the availability of maps at tram stations and online. Take note of any transfers you need along the route, and look for your departure and destination locations.

Getting On The Tram:

Stand behind the bright yellow safety line painted on the platform while you wait for the tram to arrive at your stop. This guarantees your safety as the tram approaches the stop. Allow people to get off the tram after it has stopped completely before getting on. Remember to confirm your ticket at one of the ticket validation machines after boarding the tram.

Seating Yourself And Storing Your Bags:

If the tram is busy when you board, you may take a seat or grab onto a railing or strap. There are allocated spaces in the tram to store your items if you have baggage. Check local regulations to bring your bike onboard since bicycles are only permitted on certain trams and during certain hours.

Recognizing When To Leave:

As you get closer to your destination, you'll hear announcements on the tram about the forthcoming stations. Pay attention to these announcements, and double-check your position using a map or GPS on your phone. Feel free to ask a fellow traveler or the tram driver for help if you need clarification on when to disembark.

Transferring And Leaving:

Exit the tram via the right doors when you reach your destination, ensuring care to take all your goods with you. Follow the instructions provided on the platform or refer to your map if you need to connect to another tram or another means of transportation. Most tram stations have good connections to other transit systems, allowing you to navigate Quebec easily.

Safety And Etiquette

Always be aware of regional culture and traditions when using the tram service in Quebec. Allow elderly, pregnant, or disabled people to take your seat. Reduce your volume of conversation and avoid eating or drinking on board. Above all, always adhere to the tram system's safety regulations, such as holding onto the rails when riding and staying below the yellow line while at stations.

Using this book and its practical advice on utilizing Quebec's tram system, you'll have a convenient, effective, and hassle-free time visiting the city. Additionally, when you travel on these cutting-edge trams, you'll create priceless memories and improve the environment. Travel safely and have fun while you're in Quebec!

HOW TO RIDE THE BUS SAFELY

Whether you're a native or a visitor to the charming province of Quebec, using the public transit system is economical and a great way to see the city firsthand. Finding your way around the bus system might be difficult if you've never used public transportation before or are new to the province. Do not worry; we have you covered. The purpose of this manual is to provide you with a smooth and comfortable bus traveling experience in the lovely province of Quebec.

Choosing the Correct Fare:

You must purchase the proper transport fare before starting your bus trip to Quebec. Transport authorities, route zones, and passenger eligibility (adult, student, or senior) affect bus ticket prices. To find out about fares, fare options, and points of sale, go to the website of the local transportation provider (such as RTC for Quebec City, STL for Laval, or STM for Montreal). You may purchase tickets, load a smart card, or even utilize a mobile app to pay for your fare. Choose the best fare choice for your trip needs.

Create a Route:

Planning your route is essential to guarantee hassle-free and seamless bus travel. The websites, smartphone apps, or printed schedules available at key transit hubs of the individual transport provider provide access to Quebec bus timetables and routes.

Alternatively, you may plan your trip using Google Maps by inputting your starting location, destination, and preferred arrival time. You are acquainted with bus numbers, stops, transfer spots, and timetables to ensure understanding.

Arrive Early at the Bus Stop:

Once you've determined your route, arrive at the bus stop a few minutes before the bus arrives. This enables you to choose a decent waiting area and guarantees that you will get it if the bus comes early. In Quebec, bus stations often have the bus route number and timetable displayed so that you may confirm the details as you wait.

Paying your fare and boarding the bus:

Verify the bus's display for the right route number as it draws near to prevent confusion. Passengers enter the bus at the front door in Quebec. Always wait for passengers to depart the bus before entering. Pay your fare at the entrance by placing cash or tickets in the fare box, putting your smart card into the card reader, or giving the driver your mobile app ticket. After paying your fee, ask the driver for a transfer if you need one.

Find a Seat and Take It Easy:

After paying your price, go on to a seat if available. If it's not essential, avoid priority seating, which is set aside for elderly and disabled customers. If you carry baggage or other bulky things, keep them close without blocking the aisle or in designated storage areas. Enjoy the scenery as you travel through Quebec's lovely neighborhoods and streets.

Getting Off the Bus:

You'll need to request your stop in advance, so pay careful attention to the bus stops as they approach. Most buses in Quebec feature a yellow pull cord or strip that passengers must push or pull to let the driver know they wish to get off at the next stop. It will be clear if a light, buzzer, or bell has recognized the stop request. Before getting up and moving toward the exit door, often found towards the bus's rear, wait until the vehicle has stopped.

Once you are acquainted with the transportation system in

Quebec, using the bus may be a snap. Always remember to show consideration for your fellow travelers, follow the bus's regulations, and behave properly. This guide will ensure that your bus trip is fun and comfortable and that you get the most out of your travels in Quebec.

DIRECTIONS TO
THE AIRPORT

Your travel experience in Quebec may depend on how you get to the airport. Consider the many transportation alternatives available and choose the one that best meets your requirements and tastes to guarantee a pleasant and stress-free journey. Here is a detailed instruction on visiting the Quebec airport like a native.

Selecting the proper airport:

Before anything else, remember that the province of Quebec has two airports: Montreal-Trudeau International Airport (YUL) and Quebec City Jean-Lesage International Airport (YQB). Quebec City's airport is smaller but provides a variety of local and international connections, unlike Montreal's, which is busier and acts as a hub for domestic and international flights. Verify your departure airport and make travel arrangements if necessary.

International Airport of Montreal-Trudeau (YUL)

You have a variety of alternatives for getting to Montreal-Trudeau International Airport (YUL), so you can choose one that fits your interests and budget. These consist of the following:

1. Public transportation: The 747 Express Bus, which connects downtown Montreal's Berri-UQAM station with the airport, is run by the Société de Transport de Montréal (STM). Buses operate continuously every 30 minutes, making it a practical and

affordable choice. Coins may be used to pay the fee for the 747 bus on board, or you can buy a ticket from the automated machines at the metro station. Please keep your receipt if you must show it throughout your travel, so don't lose it.

2. Taxis and ridesharing services, such as Uber and Lyft, are accessible all throughout the city if you'd want a more relaxing trip. Taxi fares from downtown Montreal to the airport might vary, but you should budget around CAD 40. Rideshares may be booked using the corresponding applications on your smartphone and are often more economical.

3. Airport shuttles are provided by several hotels and off-site parking facilities at Montreal-Trudeau International Airport (YUL). Ask about airport transport services before booking your hotel since they could be included or extra depending on where you stay.

4. Drive and park: If you have a lot of baggage or are going with family, driving to the airport and parking your vehicle may be a practical choice. Several parking alternatives are available at the airport, including short-term, multi-level, and inexpensive lots. Remember that parking costs may rapidly increase, so make financial preparations and book your space.

Airport Jean-Lesage International (YQB) in Quebec

The number of ways to get to Quebec City Jean-Lesage International Airport (YQB) has decreased, but you should still be able to locate an efficient means of transportation:

1. Public Transportation: The 76, 80, or 81 lines of the Réseau de transport de la Capitale (RTC) are a few bus routes that may get you to the airport. However, plan your journey using the RTC travel planner if you need to transfer. Keep in mind that those with light bags should use public transportation.

2. Taxis and ridesharing services like Uber are a practical way to get to the Quebec City airport. Depending on where in the city you are starting from, the cost of a taxi to the airport might vary from $34 to CAD 40. Similar to Montreal, rideshares are often less expensive.

3. Drive and Park: The Jean-Lesage International Airport (YQB) in

Quebec City provides visitors with a range of parking options, including short-term, long-term, and economy lots. Make a reservation for your venue in advance and be prepared to budget for associated costs.

Always consider your spending limit, personal preferences, and point of departure while organizing your journey to the Quebec airport. Although inexpensive, there are better choices than public transportation. While driving and airport shuttles may be more practical for folks with larger bags or families, taxis and rideshares provide a pleasant means of transportation. Whichever route you use, give yourself plenty of time to account for traffic and other possible delays to ensure a stress-free departure from Quebec.

QUEBEC'S PRIME TRAVEL SEASON

Whil organizing a vacation to Quebec might be thrilling, choosing the best time to go is essential for having the best possible experience. Quebec is home to various landscapes, vibrant cities, and various seasonal activities that appeal to various interests. This guide will provide insightful information on the best time to visit Quebec based on your tastes, financial situation, and chosen activities.

Seasonal Summary

Quebec has four unique seasons, each with its allure, celebrations, and attractions. Although late spring to early autumn is considered the finest time to visit Quebec, let's look at each season to help you decide which is right.

Spring (March to May): For those who love the outdoors and wish to see the rebirth of the local flora and animals, spring may be a revitalizing season to go to Quebec. You'll find many flowers blossoming at this time of year, and the weather will be pleasant. For those seeking a more serene experience, spring might be less congested than summer.

Summer (June to August): Visitors to Quebec like to travel during the summer because of the warm weather, the abundance of outdoor activities, and the exciting events. Travelers may partake in various activities at this time, including kayaking, hiking, and cycling. The summer season presents a wealth of outdoor concerts, street performances, and festivities honoring the Quebecois spirit for cultural enthusiasts.

Fall (September to November): Quebec is home to some of the world's most beautiful fall foliage. Photographers, hikers, and tourists who prefer milder temperatures are drawn to the woods and parks by the kaleidoscope of hues. Fall is also the season to enjoy Quebec's harvest, a gastronomic delicacy made with apples, squash, and pumpkins that are grown nearby. Visits to cider mills and wineries are great ways to take advantage of the finest of the season.

Winter (December to February): For those who like the cold and winter activities, Quebec's winter wonderland is ideal. Winter sports lovers may enjoy snowshoeing, skiing, and snowboarding, to name a few. If you want to travel at this time, you must go to the famed Quebec Winter Carnival, typically held in February.

Festivals and Events: The ideal time to visit Quebec may depend on the events and festivals that are scheduled there; these events and festivals appeal to various interests.

Popular choices to think about include:

1. Montreal Jazz Festival (June to July): Every year, music enthusiasts from all over the globe travel to Montreal to participate in this Festival, which has a variety of shows over ten days that include top international performers and local artists.

2. The world's biggest comedy festival, Just For Laughs Festival, is in Montreal in July. Thousands of comedians entertain audiences all around the city.

3. The Quebec City Summer Festival, which takes place in July, is a well-liked occasion that draws tourists to Quebec during the hot summer months. It is well-known for its varied programming. The event features outdoor performances, cuisine, and live music.

4. Winter Carnival, Quebec City (February): This Festival, one of the biggest in the world, lasts two weeks and features thrilling activities for people of all ages, including parades, snow

sculptures, ice skating, and evening celebrations.

CONSIDERATIONS FOR TRAVEL AND WEATHER

The weather in Quebec from late spring to early October is often nice and suited for outdoor activities, despite the chance for the occasional shower. Budgetary considerations are crucial when deciding when to visit since traveling during the peak season may increase lodging costs.

one may enjoy Quebec's various charms throughout the year, with each season providing a distinctive range of activities and attractions. Plan your vacation considering the festivals, events, and activities that are essential to you. Above all, no matter when you come, immerse yourself in Quebec's lively culture, breathtaking scenery, and kind hospitality.

The best time to visit depends on the kind of visitor.

With its stunning natural surroundings, charming historical architecture, and the fusion of Francophone and Anglophone cultures, a journey to Quebec may be a spectacular experience. This information will assist all sorts of visitors—from those who like the outdoors and exploring cities to those who enjoy festivals and winter sports—in determining the ideal time to visit Quebec. With the proper knowledge, you can organize the ideal vacation that fits your travel preferences and interests.

Nature lovers: enjoy the splendor of the changing seasons

Quebec has wonderful natural surroundings, from majestic rivers and national parks to lovely woods and whale-watching locations. If you like the outdoors, you should visit Quebec in the early autumn (September to October) and late spring (May to June). These times of year provide nice, warm weather, brilliant natural colors, and little tourist activity. With the foliage's shifting hues, fall is especially beautiful. Visit places like Tadoussac, Forillon National Park, and Parc National de la Jacques-Cartier for a once-in-a-lifetime adventure.

City Explorers: Exploring the culture of the city

Plan your trip between late spring and early autumn to enjoy Quebec's charming cities and urban landscapes. In the summer (June to August), the streets come alive when sidewalk cafés, boutiques, and cultural activities are in full flow. Montreal and Quebec City are ideal places to visit since they are rich in history, fine art, and stunning architecture. As a UNESCO World Heritage site with cobblestone lanes and buildings from the 17th century, Old Quebec City is a must-see.

Festival lovers embrace the spirit of celebration.

Throughout the year, Quebec is renowned for hosting many top-notch festivals and events. If you prefer attending festivals, you'll appreciate traveling to Quebec between June and August, when the province exhibits its vibrant vitality via various activities. Among the interesting events to anticipate is the Montgolfières hot air balloon festival in Saint-Jean-sur-Richelieu, the Just for Laughs Comedy Festival, the Quebec City Summer Festival, and the Montreal Jazz Festival. During the festival season, it is advised to reserve lodging in advance since it might become quite crowded.

FOR LOVERS OF WINTER SPORTS, VISIT QUEBEC'S WINTER PARADISE.

If you love participating in winter sports and activities, you'll be excited to explore everything Quebec offers from December through February. This lovely region turns into a snowy wonderland during the winter, offering chances for skiing, snowboarding, snowshoeing, dog sledding, and even ice climbing. For fans of winter sports, Quebec's ski resorts, such as Mont-Tremblant and Mont-Sainte-Anne, provide memorable experiences. The annual Winter Carnival, which takes place in early February and provides a unique and joyous environment, is when Québec City, particularly, comes to life.

Finally, your hobbies and travel choices will determine the perfect time to visit Quebec. Visit during the pleasant late spring and early autumn months if you love nature. Urban explorers should visit the province during the hot summer months, while festival goers will appreciate it from June through August. Last but not least, if you like snow activities or wish to experience the Quebec Winter Carnival, go throughout the winter, from December to February. Whatever time of year you decide to come there, Quebec is a mesmerizing location that ensures an amazing trip.

BEST TIME TO VISIT FOR TRAVELERS ON A BUDGET

A backpacker's paradise, Quebec is a beautiful province in eastern Canada. The province provides a range of experiences that would make any traveler fall in love with the area thanks to its distinctive combination of contemporary metropolitan life and timeless elegance dating back centuries. But when is the ideal time to go by backpack to Quebec? We have included useful information in this guide to assist you in making travel arrangements and maximizing your time in Quebec.

April to June: "Spring Brilliance"

Quebec wakes to a beautiful season for the ideal hiking trip as the snow melts and the temperatures start to climb. Exploring the many towns and paths in the province is made possible by the blossoming trees, the verdant scenery, and the nice weather. The yearly sugar shack ritual, where you may indulge in delectable maple syrup products while taking in the province's distinctive culture, is best experienced in the spring.

Summer's Beauty (June through August)

The best time to go to Quebec is undoubtedly between June through August during the summer. The pleasant weather gives you the chance to participate in various outdoor pursuits like cycling and hiking while also allowing you to attend Quebec's exciting festivals. Enjoy the captivating cultural activities of the First Peoples Festival in Montreal, participate in the famous Montreal Jazz Festival, and see astounding street performers at the Festival d'été de Québec.

(September – November) Fall Charm

The months of September through November are your best choice if you want to go backpacking through stunning landscapes covered with autumn color. The weather is warm throughout this time, making it ideal for taking in Quebec's beautiful outdoors and old streets. Discover a variety of autumn festivities, including the Montreal World Film Festival, and take in Quebec's spectacular Fall colors through parks, rivers, and scenic routes.

(December – March) Winter Wonderland

Winter in Quebec may be the ideal season to travel if you're a daring and adventure-seeking traveler. Despite the freezing weather and copious amounts of snow, this time of year turns the province into a winter paradise with many activities to suit your snowy fantasies. There is no lack of fun to be had in Quebec during the chilly months, from skiing and snowboarding in the Laurentians or Eastern Townships to visiting the famous Winter Carnival in Quebec City.

Your tastes, interests, and travel objectives determine the ideal time to visit Quebec. From the spring's flowering sceneries to the winter's thrills in the snow, each season has something special to offer to satisfy the needs of the contemporary traveler. Whenever you decide to visit Quebec, you can count on its rich cultural experiences, spectacular natural beauty, and friendly people to enchant your mind and heart.

WHEN TO GO ON A HONEYMOON?

Q uebec, a charming Canadian province, is a great honeymoon location for couples looking for romance, excitement, and a touch of European flair. Consider the ideal time to visit Quebec as you prepare for your special holiday to ensure an outstanding experience. To help you make the most of your honeymoon, we'll examine the many seasons, sites, and activities ideal for varied tastes in this guide.

Honeymoon in the Winter: December to February

Quebec is ideal for your honeymoon if you and your companion want to enjoy a winter paradise. Cities and landscapes transform into a mystical, snow-covered wonderland during this time of year. The legendary Québec Winter Carnival and the German Christmas Market in Quebec City are both must-attend events that will make your trip merry. For those who like winter sports, the province has some ski resorts where you can hit the slopes and participate in snow-related activities like snowboarding, ice skating, and snowshoeing. Quebec's winter season offers beautiful snowfall and more affordable hotel prices, making it a great option for couples looking for a snug, romantic retreat.

March to May: Spring Honeymoon

Quebec comes to life in the spring when the snow melts, and

the weather rises. Couples that like warmer weather and fewer people should go during this season. The area's natural beauty comes to life with colorful flowers and lush vegetation, providing a magnificent setting for strolls and outdoor meals. This is a terrific opportunity to take your time and leisurely visit the historical landmarks, art galleries, and museums in Quebec City and Montreal. Additionally, when fewer visitors are around, you can often find affordable lodging and attend cultural events and festivals like the Montreal Digital Spring and the Québec City Magic Festival.

June to August: Summer Honeymoon

The summer is the best time to go to Quebec for couples looking for warmth and bright days. The province comes to life with vibrant festivals, outdoor performances, and busy patios that energize and revitalize the cities. Enjoy this season's gorgeous scenery by taking a scenic drive through the Charlevoix area or a romantic whale-watching cruise along the St. Lawrence River. During this season, it is ideal to go trekking, camping and taking in Canada's natural marvels in Quebec's National Parks, such as Forillon and La Mauricie. But keep in mind that it's often tourist season's busiest time, so hotel costs and crowd levels may increase.

Honeymoon in the Fall: September to November

Quebec's autumn is a stunning display of colorful foliage and crisp, chilly air. This season is ideal for couples who want to enjoy Quebec's charm in a tranquil and stunning environment. In locations like Jacques-Cartier National Park, Mount Royal Park, and Île d'Orléans, the autumn foliage offers a beautiful setting for romantic picnics, strolls, and picture ops. As the weather becomes colder, festivals and cultural events abound in the cities, like the Quebec City Celtic Festival and the Montreal World Film Festival. Fall unquestionably gives a private, enchanted honeymoon experience since there are fewer visitors and nicer weather.

The perfect time to go on your honeymoon to Quebec ultimately relies on your particular choices and the kind of experience you're looking for. Quebec provides a choice of sights and activities to make your honeymoon a remarkable vacation, from enchanted winter escapes to vibrant summer festivals. Prepare to make lifelong memories with your special someone in this beautiful Canadian province by taking into account your chosen weather, hobbies, and spending limit.

THE SEASONAL PEAK IN QUEBEC

Quebec, a popular tourist destination noted for its varied terrain and Euro-American flair, is a place that provides life-changing events throughout the year. However, at its busiest time, this Canadian province exhibits its finest qualities and draws visitors worldwide. This guide will walk you through what to anticipate, experience, and enjoy when visiting Quebec during the busy season.

Summer: A Time for Celebrations and Outdoor Activities

Quebec's summer season, which lasts from June through August, is distinguished by pleasant weather, exciting events, and a wide range of outdoor activities. The province's natural beauty may be explored in a climate that ranges from 20°C to 30°C during this period.

The Festival d'été de Québec, a ten-day music extravaganza involving worldwide musicians, is the most well-known summertime festival. The famous jazz festival, which features local and international talent, is also held in Montreal. The Fête Nationale, which takes place on June 24, also honors the Francophone history of several Quebec communities.

The mild weather offers a wonderful chance to discover Quebec's breathtaking scenery. In its many provincial parks, the summer is a great time for hiking, mountain biking, or canoeing.

Additionally, this time of year is excellent for whale viewing on the St. Lawrence River, where you can see belugas, humpbacks, and blue whales.

Autumn: A Season of Color and Harvest Festivals

Quebec enjoys autumn, a great season when the province is painted in beautiful red, orange, and yellow tones from September to November. Temperatures range from 5 to 15 degrees Celsius on average over the season.

Visitors may enjoy the stunning sight of Quebec's foliage at this time by going for a picturesque drive around the countryside or hiking in national parks like La Mauricie and Mont-Tremblant. When the leaves change colors, the cobblestone streets of Quebec City, particularly, take on a special appeal.

Fall also brings a variety of harvest-themed activities, such as apple picking in the area's numerous orchards or visiting wineries in the Eastern Townships. The Gardens of Light in Montreal provide Chinese lanterns to light the gloomy nights.

Winter: An Enchanting Winter Wonderland

The province of Quebec is transformed into a lovely snowy wonderland during the peak winter months of December to February. During this period, the temperature might fall below freezing and even as low as –20 °C.

Despite the extreme cold, Quebec winters are filled with amazing encounters. The famed Québec Winter Carnival occurs from late January to mid-February, and the province is illuminated with Christmas markets. Skiing, snowboarding, snowshoeing, and even an exhilarating snowmobile safari are available to outdoor lovers.

Any winter travel plan must include stops at the enchanting Hôtel de Glace and the German Christmas Market in Québec City. Additionally, relaxing with a hot beverage after a day of snowy activities is a special pleasure.

Spring: A Time for New Beginnings and Rebirth

Quebec's spring season, with temperatures ranging from 5°C to 20°C, emerges as the snow melts from March through May. The region is less crowded at this time of year, which is perfect for a more contemplative and tranquil journey.

Spring is a great time to visit Québec City's numerous parks or the botanical gardens in Montreal to see cherry blossoms and tulips in bloom. Use the shoulder season to avoid the busy crowds and visit Quebec's well-known urban regions like Old Québec and the Plateau Mont-Royal.

The busiest time of year in Quebec provides a variety of activities to suit every traveler's preferences. This beautiful Canadian region offers something for everyone, from exciting summer events to winter wonderland excursions. Pack your luggage and go to Quebec during one of its most enchanted seasons for an experience you will remember.

SPROUTING IN QUEBEC

A visit to Quebec in the spring will delight your senses as the winter frost fades and the countryside begins to come alive with bright hues. This large Canadian province is home to diverse activities, a huge wilderness, a rich cultural history, and delectable food. Here is the definitive guide to enjoying Quebec's grandeur in the rejuvenating embrace of spring.

Take Part in the Festivals
Numerous events take place around the province in the spring. A leisurely afternoon stroll is made possible by Sherbrooke's Fête des Tulipes, a tulip festival that blankets the town with a million blooming tulips in late April. May sees Festival TransAmériques take over Montreal's theaters and streets with its performances of modern dance. During La Fête de la Pomme, the Montérégie region's flowering apple orchards will delight your taste buds with some of the greatest apple-based treats.

Enjoy Nature's Blessings
One of the finest times to see Quebec's tremendous biodiversity is in the spring when migrating birds return to their breeding areas and the greenery blossoms. Visit Mont-Tremblant National Park for a gratifying dose of nature, where hiking and canoeing options

abound among beautiful scenery. Another must-visit place is the Îles de la Madeleine, which provides a distinctive experience with its gorgeous red cliffs, sloping dunes, and lovely coastlines.

Unwind in the urban slums.

The cities of Quebec provide a remarkable mix of past, present, and gastronomic delights. When visiting Quebec City, the birthplace of French America, in the spring, you may stroll through the old town's flower-lined cobblestone streets. The outdoor patios of bustling cafés in Montreal provide chances to enjoy the city's vibrant energy and sample its varied cuisine for a more international experience. Go for a walk along the Lachine Canal or unwind at one of the many picnic areas scattered around Mount Royal Park.

Experience a Road Trip

As the snow melts and the colors of the countryside emerge in the spring, the province's picturesque drives are a treat. Wine lovers may enjoy a range of regional vintages along the Route des Vins in the Eastern Townships. The Gaspe Peninsula can be reached by car and offers breathtaking coastline vistas, little fishing towns, and Percé Rock and Forillon National Park sights.

Get Moving

Quebec offers a variety of unique and fascinating ways to experience the province throughout the spring. Cycling is a fun way to explore the area and is quite popular among the residents. Take a bike ride along the coastline trail at Parc National du Bic or through the beautiful landscapes and peaceful communities of the Petit Train du Nord Linear Park. Golf complexes, fishing possibilities, and horseback riding paths are widely available in Quebec and provide a wonderful opportunity to experience the outdoors.

For all types of travelers, spring in Quebec is a season bursting with revitalization, events, and activities that provide great travel experiences. Quebec in spring is an adventure waiting to happen, whether you wish to get lost in nature, join people in exciting festivals, or tour the busy cities.

SUMMERTIME
IN QUEBEC

The best time to visit Quebec is during the summer when you can take advantage of the buzzing towns, picturesque countryside, and exciting festivities that take place then. This travel guide will provide the advice, suggestions, and knowledge you need to make the most of your summer vacation in Quebec.

Investigate Quebec City:

Quebec City, a UNESCO World Heritage site renowned for its old-world beauty and interesting history, is a great place to start your journey across Quebec. Stroll around Old Quebec's cobblestone alleys to discover charming restaurants, inviting cafés, and charming stores offering regional handicrafts. A must-see attraction, the majestic Château Frontenac has beautiful riverbank vistas and elaborate designs. To learn more about the city's fascinating history, take a guided walking tour or ride in a horse-drawn carriage.

Discover Montreal:

The biggest city in Quebec, Montreal, provides the ideal fusion of contemporary lifestyle with a French flair. The city comes alive in the summer with many outdoor activities, art exhibits, and culinary festivals. Explore the cobblestone alleyways of Old Montreal or go to the hip Mile End area for unique stores and green parks. Remember to climb Mont-Royal to its highest point for sweeping views of the city's skyline.

Discover the Beauty of Nature:

The natural marvels of Quebec's countryside are begging to be discovered. Consider taking a day trip to Montmorency Falls to see the thundering waterfall that drops from a height much higher than Niagara Falls. Another fantastic location with verdant fields and charming towns evoking rural France is Ile d'Orleans. Visit Saguenay Fjord National Park in the north for hiking, kayaking, and whale viewing in a more natural environment.

Participate in Events and Festivals:

The season is complete by participating in the many festivals held throughout the summer in Quebec. The Montreal International Jazz Festival is a well-known occasion featuring top performers in various settings. The biggest comedy festival in the world, Just For Laughs, offers nonstop giggles with stand-up artists and street entertainment. At the same time, significant worldwide bands are drawn to Quebec City's event d'été de Québec, a multi-genre music event that lasts for many days.

Take Advantage of Culinary Delights:

Prepare to be completely engrossed in Quebec's delectable combination of French and regional cuisine. Eat Quebec's famous comfort cuisine and poutine, or choose a luxurious dinner at a farm-to-table restaurant that uses foods grown nearby. Innumerable places in Québec's microbrewery sector, which features inventive craft brews and distinctive tastes, are also not to be missed.

Visit the Eastern Townships to relax:

Go to the Eastern Townships, halfway between Montreal and Quebec City, if you want to unwind. There are stunning scenery, vineyards, and attractive towns in the area. Visit the well-known town of Magog, which is situated on the coast of Lake Memphremagog. Here, you may go boating, relax on the beach, and eat by the lake. North Hatley, renowned for its scenic landscape and population of young artists, is another lovely location.

All sorts of tourists should visit Quebec in the summer. Throughout your trip to Quebec, you'll have several possibilities to make lifetime memories thanks to the province's numerous cities, breathtaking natural wonders, exciting festivals, and distinctive gastronomic experiences. Plan your vacation now and prepare to be enchanted by Quebec's summer enchantment.

QUEBEC IN THE FALL

As the summer heat fades, Canada's biggest province dons its most gorgeous hues, providing a bright background for visitors interested in learning more about the region's dynamic culture, delectable cuisine, and fascinating history. Embrace the allure of Quebec's golden season with our comprehensive guide to taking advantage of the province's finest in the fall, whether you're a first-time tourist or a frequent visitor with a soft spot for the leaves.

Montreal, a city that is bursting with creativity and history, is a place that is best explored in the autumn. The city's colorful districts are ideal for strolls since the streets are covered with shades of red, orange, and yellow. Begin your adventure in Old Montreal, where you may take in the majestic Notre Dame Basilica and explore Place Jacques-Cartier. The Lachine Canal, where the colors highlight the shoreline, and the well-known Mount Royal Park, where you can see some of the city's most stunning vistas surrounded by vegetation, are not to be missed.

Fantastic food festivals and culinary events are also held in Montreal throughout the autumn. Highlights include the Olympic Stadium's First Fridays food truck spectacular and the Oysterfest, where you may satisfy your oyster appetites.

With a visit to the province's namesake city, a journey to Quebec in the fall is complete. As the leaves change color around you, Old Quebec's lovely cobblestone streets will transport you back in time. To experience the history of Old Quebec, a UNESCO World

Heritage site, begin in Place Royale, the cradle of French America. If you like stunning landscapes, Montmorency Falls Park is a must-see short distance from the city. The sparkling waterfall, framed by the rusty splendor of the season, will astound you.

In September, Quebec City also plays home to the Grand Prix Cycliste de Quebec, a world-famous competition for cyclists and sports fans. Check out the Great Color Adventure at the close-by Mont-Sainte-Anne resort for mountain biking, chairlift rides, and various other outdoor activities that honor Quebec's steep fall.

Hire a vehicle and go on a beautiful road trip to find some of Quebec's most beautiful undiscovered jewels. The Gaspésie Tour, where you can see the vibrant coastline alongside attractive coastal towns, and the Eastern Townships, a region famed for its charming villages, wineries, and magnificent scenery, are just a few of the prominent itineraries.

Quebec is amid its harvest season and abundantly clear everywhere you go. Don't miss the Apple Festival in Monteregie, which showcases the area's most popular fruit, or the Oktoberfest des Québécois in Repentigny, modeled after the German celebration. Attend the annual La Fête du Chocolat de Bromont, a chocolate festival with seminars, tastings, and other chocolaty treats, if you're in the mood for something sweet.

Consider scheduling a tranquil train trip through the countryside or a picturesque river cruise along the St. Lawrence River for a unique viewpoint on Quebec's autumn splendor. The regional rail service Orford Express and an AML Croisières boat are wonderful ways to take in the magnificence of Quebec in October in a comfortable and laid-back atmosphere.

Quebec in the fall is a kaleidoscope of colors, fun celebrations, and breathtaking scenery. La Belle Province's visually exciting season will undoubtedly make a lasting impression on your memory, inspiring you to come back and discover more of what this magnificent Canadian province has to offer. As you go off on your wonderful autumn tour across Quebec, take your sweater, camera, and spirit of adventure.

WINTER IN QUEBEC

Quebec becomes a wonderful landscape out of a novel as winter draws near and the snow falls. From the glittering Quebec Winter Carnival to the breathtaking scenery of its national parks, this French-Canadian province offers a variety of enthralling experiences. There is no other destination quite like Quebec for those looking for the ideal winter getaway. In this travel guide, we'll explore Quebec's various wintertime splendors, emphasizing must-see sights and providing advice on how to make the most of your trip.

Without a stay in Quebec City, the province's bustling capital, no trip to Quebec in the winter would be complete. The city offers a stunning winter picture with snow-covered streets, glistening holiday lights, and the imposing Fairmont Le Château Frontenac rising above. Visit Old Quebec's cobblestone alleyways for a romantic promenade and the historic Petit-Champlain neighborhood, renowned for its European ambiance and boutique stores. Make sure to visit one of the charming cafés or bistros to sample some regional specialties like poutine, tarte au sucre, and tourtière.

One of the most eagerly awaited events of the year is the Quebec Winter Carnival, which occurs every year between the end of January and the middle of February. Ice carving, snow rafting, and a stunning night parade with extravagant floats, costumed characters, and energetic entertainment will let you embrace your inner kid. Of course, seeing the jovial, snowman-like Bonhomme

Carnaval, the festival's renowned mascot, is a must if you want to experience winter in Quebec. You won't want to forget this once-in-a-lifetime adventure, so remember your camera.

The ideal time to discover Quebec's natural beauty is during the winter via national parks. Just thirty minutes north of Quebec, visit Jacques-Cartier National Park.

Observe the city's breathtaking glacier valleys, flowing rivers, and snow-covered woodlands. Enjoy cross-country skiing, snowshoeing, or a thrilling dogsledding journey through the untouched forest on its scenic pathways. Mont-Tremblant National Place, which has a famous ski resort and spectacular frozen waterfalls, is another place that must be seen.

Quebec is a snow sports enthusiast's paradise with over 75 ski resorts and top-notch skiing. Mont Tremblant has the highest height in eastern North America, providing the best skiing and snowboarding conditions and a wide range of après-ski activities. Visit Le Massif de Charlevoix, renowned for its dangerous descents and off-trail skiing chances, for a more adventurous getaway.

After a day of visiting Quebec's winter splendor, warm and opulent lodgings will help you unwind. The Fairmont Le Château Frontenac in Quebec City offers luxurious accommodations with breathtaking views and is conveniently near key attractions. Consider reserving a stay in a charming mountain lodge or a Scandinavian-style chalet for a more private and distant experience.

Quebec offers a wide range of unusual seasonal activities as a winter playground. Visit the Hotel de Glace, a beautiful ice hotel equipped with ice sculptures, an ice bar, and even ice beds, or try ice fishing on one of the numerous frozen lakes in the area. Visit the Village Vacances Valcartier for an even more exhilarating experience and participate in the exhilarating snow tubing and ice-sliding activities there.

Travel Advice for Quebec in the Winter:

Wear layers of insulating materials like fleece, moisture-wicking textiles, and waterproof clothing to remain warm and dry.

- Take your time while exploring to avoid ice areas and tricky situations.

- Think about hiring a vehicle to get the most out of your winter excursion. However, be ready for snowy and slippery roads by bringing a winter safety kit and following winter driving safety recommendations.

Quebec is a fantastic location for a winter getaway because of its beautiful scenery, thrilling winter activities, and festive charm. Quebec in the winter is a magnificent paradise, whether you're planning a romantic trip, an outdoor adventure, or a family holiday. So wear warm clothing, grab snow boots, and discover Quebec's wintertime charm.

A GUIDE TO VISITING QUEBEC MONTH BY MONTH

T he province of Quebec is home to dynamic cities, breathtaking landscapes, and a rich cultural past, making travel there a really unique experience. Unique events, activities, and attractions are available every month of the year. This guide will give you an idea of what to anticipate and help you get the most out of your trip to Quebec whenever you go.

January:

In Quebec, January marks the beginning of winter. Put on your warmest clothes and take in Quebec City's famed Québec Winter Carnival, one of the world's biggest and oldest winter festivities. This experience is wonderful due to the ice palaces, snow sculptures, night parades, and outdoor performances. The Laurentians and Eastern Townships ski resorts are open to skiers and snowboarders.

February:

With the Montréal en Lumière festival in February, tourists may continue to enjoy wintertime activities outside and in the arts. This month is especially ideal for seeing the amazing ice formations at the Parc de la Chute-Montmorency or ice skating on one of the numerous outdoor rinks in Quebec's cities.

March:

The sugar shack season starts as winter draws to a close. Discover how maple syrup is produced traditionally in Quebec and processed into delectable sweets like sugar on snow (tire sur la neige). Before the snow disappears, outdoor enthusiasts may still go skiing, snowshoeing, and dog sledding.

April:

Quebec experiences a riot of color and milder temperatures when spring finally arrives in April. Visit the Montreal Botanical Garden to see the stunning tulip displays and take advantage of the yearly guided birding trips. The Festival International du Film sur l'Art (FIFA), which features films that highlight the art world, is a great place for movie fans to visit.

May:

Quebec is a wonderful place to visit in May since the moderate weather and the peak travel season has yet to start. Use the uncrowded national parks like Forillon and La Mauricie this month to go hiking, biking, or camping. Take part in the thriving music scene in Montreal as the annual Pouzza Fest, an outdoor punk rock concert, takes place.

June:

The festival season officially begins in June, and one of the most well-known events is Montreal's Festival TransAmériques, which features modern performing arts. Another highlight is the famed Montreal Beer Fest, where you may taste regional and foreign breweries. During this season, whales migrate back to the St. Lawrence River, providing chances for whale-watching trips.

July:

Numerous events occur in July, such as Canada Day and the renowned Montreal Jazz Festival. The biggest worldwide comedy festival, Just for Laughs, is to be noticed. Visit Quebec's "Via Ferrata" or Iron Roads, a combination of trekking and rock climbing at picturesque spots like Mont Tremblant and Parc Aventures Cap Jaseux, if you're looking for some outdoor thrills.

August:

August is the height of summer in Quebec. Visit one of the

stunning beaches on the Gaspé Peninsula or Île d'Orléans to take advantage of the warm weather and sunny days. During culinary festivals or the many farmers' markets spread around the province, foodies may indulge in regional specialties like poutine, tourtière, and fresh fruit.

September:

September is a great month to go to Quebec because of its stunning fall foliage as autumn approaches. Take picturesque drives through the Laurentians or Eastern Townships, or go hiking in Gatineau Park, close to Ottawa. September marks the beginning of the wine harvest, and you may participate in wine tastings along the Route des Vins de Brome-Missisquoi or go to the Magdalen Islands' grape harvest celebration.

October:

The bright crimson and golden tones of Quebec's autumn leaves are best seen in October. Cycle the 200-kilometer P'tit Train du Nord bike track across the breathtaking Laurentian landscapes to make the most of this season. The Festival of Quebec Cinema, which presents the greatest films from the province, also takes place in October in Quebec City.

November:

In Quebec, November marks the change from autumn to winter. Wrap up and explore Montreal's many art exhibits, such as the yearly Montreal Biennial, or explore its museums of culture and history. Wildlife lovers should go to the Saguenay-St. Visit Lawrence Marine Park to see belugas and seals on their way to wintering grounds.

December:

Quebec is very beautiful in December, when the cities are decorated with sparkling lights and the streets are coated with snow. Attend seasonal activities like the Nutcracker Ballet in Montreal or the German Christmas Market in Quebec City to celebrate the season. Book a stay at the Hôtel de Glace, a one-of-a-kind ice hotel close to Quebec City, for an exceptional experience.

Quebec has many occasions, chances, and activities throughout the year that appeal to all preferences and interests. This guide will assist you in getting the most out of your trip to Quebec throughout any month of the year, whether you want to see the colorful foliage or take in the province's rich cultural legacy.

QUEBEC ESSENTIALS TO PACK

I t's crucial to consider Quebec's varied temperature, activities, and culture while making travel plans to ensure you pack everything you'll need for your trip. It's crucial to be ready since this dynamic Canadian province offers a variety of experiences, from busy cities to breathtaking scenery. In this advice, we'll go through the necessities for packing so you may have an enjoyable and stress-free vacation to Quebec.

I. Think About The Weather

Check the weather prediction for your vacation before packing your baggage since Quebec's weather may vary significantly throughout the year. The following general recommendations depend on the season:

a. Winter (December to February): The winters in Quebec are chilly, with lows of -20°C (-4°F). Pack layers of thermal clothes, insulated jackets, wool socks, gloves, caps, and scarves, among other warm accessories. In the event of snowfall, waterproof and insulated footwear will also be required.

b. Although the weather in Quebec is famously variable, spring (March to May) and fall (September to November) provide gentler temperatures. Consider bringing long sleeve shirts, sweaters, and a lightweight waterproof jacket since layering is crucial. For walking, remember to wear proper footwear for the weather.

c. Summer (June to August): The temperatures throughout the summer months in Quebec range from 20°C to 30°C (68°F to 86°F). Bring breathable, lightweight clothes like shorts, t-shirts, tank tops, sundresses, and a light jacket for chilly nights. Additionally advised are sun hats, sunglasses, and sunscreen.

Ii. Select The Proper Baggage

The amount of baggage you bring should be determined by the length of your vacation, your lodging, and the activities you want to do:

a. Suitcases: Use a rolling suitcase, preferably with a hard shell to guard against any possible weather difficulties, if you want to remain in Quebec for a longer period or if you like to keep all of your stuff in one location.

b. Backpacks: A backpack would be a better choice if you want to travel regularly and explore the outdoors. For the length of your journey, choose a comfortable, well-padded backpack that can accommodate fine clothes and necessities.

Iii. Bring Only The Basics

In addition to your clothes and weather-appropriate gear, take into account bringing the following things for your trip to Quebec:

a. Toiletries: Pack travel-sized versions of your toothpaste, toothbrush, body wash, deodorant, and any other personal care products you may need. Wet wipes and hand sanitizer in travel-sized bottles are also quite helpful.

b. Electronics: Remember to include your smartphone, charger, headphones, and other essential electronic equipment. If you plan on spending many hours touring, a power bank might be helpful, and if you are traveling from outside North America, you must have an international power adaptor.

c. Travel papers: Store your passport, license, tickets, and any other necessary travel papers in a location that is both secure and convenient to reach, such as a money belt or travel wallet. Additionally advised is a copy of your travel insurance and emergency contact details.

d. Bring a book, portable games, or a gadget to view movies and TV programs to pass the time on lengthy flights, trains, or pauses.

e. Snacks: Pack some non-perishable snacks like granola bars or trail mix to keep your energy levels up when traveling.

f. Other Travel Accessories: Depending on your intentions, you may include a reusable water bottle, a foldable umbrella, a travel cushion, reusable grocery or laundry bags, or even a travel pillow.

Iv. Observe The Culture Of The Area

Quebec has a distinctive culture and a large French-speaking population. While traveling in the province, it's crucial to be aware of the traditions and etiquette of the area. To converse and respect people, think about learning simple French words.

Wear modest clothing with knee and shoulder coverings while visiting places of worship or other conservative settings. Take ideas from the locals to blend in and avoid striking out as a visitor since Quebecois often dress elegantly yet sensibly.

You may pack confidently and have a wonderful vacation in this beautiful Canadian province by carefully considering the weather, activities, and cultural elements of your trip to Quebec.

HOW TO PACK FOR A TRIP TO QUEBEC

When preparing for a trip to Quebec, remember to bring everything you'll need to take advantage of the province's magnificent scenery, festivals, and poutine. It's crucial to consider the season, the activities you have planned, and Quebec's unique cultural customs when deciding what to pack for a trip there.

Start by bringing the right attire for the season you'll be there:

Pack clothes that will work in the warm, sometimes humid weather if you're going in the summer. Pack breathable, light clothing like loose shirts, shorts, skirts, and comfy sandals. Summer nights may become chilly, particularly in mountainous or coastal areas. To feel comfortable, you should also carry a light sweater or jacket.

Quebec's winters are renowned for their bitter weather and heavy snowfall. Be careful to dress in thermal or Merino wool base layers, cozy leggings, sweaters, and a down or waterproof winter coat. Remember to include caps, gloves, scarves, and footwear suitable for the conditions, such as waterproof snow boots with sturdy tread.

Be ready for fluctuating temperatures and potential rainfall while traveling in the spring and autumn. Bring a decent selection of lightweight and warm layers, a waterproof jacket, and closed-toe shoes or boots.

Always consider the activities you have planned when visiting Quebec, regardless of the time of year. Take the right equipment, such as hiking shoes and ski equipment, to participate in outdoor activities like skiing or hiking. Additionally, Quebec is well-known for its energetic festivals, so bring clothes suitable for evening performances and festivities.

Considering that Quebec is mostly a French-speaking province, carrying a French-English dictionary or downloading a translation app on your phone may be helpful. Although many locals can understand and speak English, it's always appreciated if you can attempt a few phrases in French. It also makes getting about the area more fun.

Remember that Quebec's electrical outlets operate at the North American standard of 110-120 volts and 60 Hertz, so if your electronic gadgets are incompatible, bring the proper power converter. Although most establishments take credit cards, having Canadian dollars on hand is a good idea in case of emergencies, small purchases, or tipping.

Pack travel-sized necessities for toiletries, including toothpaste, a toothbrush, body wash, shampoo, and conditioner. Bring a reusable water bottle to save plastic waste and your costs for bottled water. Tap water in Quebec is usually safe to drink. Additionally, useful items are travel-sized hand sanitizers and cleaning wipes, particularly while seeing touristy regions.

Pack your vacation essentials, including your passport, license, travel insurance information, and required visas. Keep physical and digital copies of these records if you misplace the originals.

Remember to bring a small first aid kit and prescription pills. All ointments, bandages, medicines, and prescription prescriptions should be retained in their original packaging to prevent confusion at security checkpoints.

With these practical suggestions for packing for your Quebec vacation, you'll be prepared with everything you need for a relaxing, enjoyable trip.

THE MOST USEFUL THINGS

A trip to Quebec delivers a wide range of breathtaking experiences. There is no lack of unique experiences waiting for you in this Canadian province, from the vibrant capitals of Montreal and Quebec City to the gorgeous area of Charlevoix. Consider adding these helpful things to your vacation schedule to make the most of your stay in Quebec.

1. The official language of Quebec is French; nevertheless, although English is widely spoken in metropolitan areas, you could run into linguistic difficulties in smaller towns and rural regions. You may save a lot of uncertainty and frustration by keeping a multilingual phrasebook on hand when translation isn't immediately accessible.

2. Comfortable walking shoes: Quebec welcomes you to explore with its abundance of outdoor activities and magnificent scenery. Comfortable and reliable footwear is necessary for your trip, whether exploring the cobblestone alleys of Old Quebec, hiking in the Laurentians, or participating in a whale-watching expedition in the Gaspé Peninsula.

3. Reusable water bottle: Hydration is crucial when exploring Quebec's breathtaking scenery. By eliminating plastic waste, carrying a reusable water bottle benefits the environment and guarantees that you will have access to water while exploring. In

addition, Quebec's tap water is among the world's cleanest and safest.

4. Dress in layers since Quebec's weather may change drastically in a single day, from frigid to warm. Packaging layers of clothes allows you to adapt to temperature changes without feeling uncomfortable. Choose breathable, lightweight fabrics that are simple to add or remove as necessary.

5. Quebec provides many photo-worthy events you'll want to record on your phone, so bring a portable phone charger or power bank. Thanks to a portable charger or power bank, your smartphone won't lose power during your excursion.

6. A trustworthy travel handbook: Do your research and invest in a thorough guidebook highlighting Quebec's must-see sights, unique culture, and hidden jewels. Using this resource, you can easily navigate your surroundings, improving your trip experience.

7. Although many large merchants accept credit cards from other countries, having Canadian dollars on hand for smaller purchases at neighborhood markets or shops is advantageous. Additionally, certain establishments could only take cash, particularly in rural locations.

8. Travel insurance: Although many tourists don't consider getting it, it's essential in an emergency. Travel insurance may provide reassurance and financial security in case of a medical emergency, unexpected airline cancellation, or missing baggage.

9. When traveling, picking up souvenirs and distinctive Quebecois goods in a small folding bag is simple. Make sure you don't use up all of your allowed baggage on your return journey by packing a compact, lightweight bag to hold your discovered treasures.

10. The most important "item" you should bring with you on your trip to Quebec is an open mind and a sense of adventure. Prepare to savor the province's delectable food, rich culture, and fascinating history. Allow yourself to be surrounded by the beautiful scenery and friendly people that make up Quebec's true appeal.

Incorporating these helpful elements into your planning for a vacation to Quebec will greatly improve your whole experience. Prepare to be enthralled by Quebec's culture, history, and stunning landscape as you experience the province's unique charm. With these valuable goods and a curious attitude along for the ride, your journey will be memorable. Take pleasure in your travels in Quebec!

CAN YOU VISIT QUEBEC SAFELY?

S afety is always a top priority for travelers regarding vacation preparation. Quebec has grown to be a well-liked travel destination for people from all over the globe because of its distinctive blend of European elegance, contemporary culture, and natural beauty. It is important to assess the current safety situation in Quebec and the safety measures needed to guarantee a worry-free and pleasurable trip. This page will provide a current review of safety conditions in Quebec in a friendly manner, concentrating on issues like crime rates, health risks, and safety advice.

Tourist Security Measures

Fortunately, Quebec is generally regarded as a safe destination. Quebec has comparatively low crime rates when compared to other popular tourist locations. The province is a welcome destination for travelers since it is multicultural and tolerant. As in any place, vigilance must still be used, and basic safety procedures must be followed. The following advice can help you stay safe when traveling across Quebec:

1. Despite the rarity of violent crime in Quebec, pickpocketing and other forms of theft may sometimes happen, especially in densely

populated tourist destinations. Keep your possessions safe, and put important papers like your passport and identification in the hotel safe.

2. Use trustworthy taxi services to travel safely; there have been allegations of scams using unregistered drivers. Be cautious while utilizing public transportation or ride-sharing services, and avoid going alone late at night.

3. The emergency number in Quebec is 911. Be aware of this number. Research the non-emergency phone numbers for the neighborhood police and hospitals, and save this one on your phone.

Health Risks And Safety Precautions

Additionally, travelers should be informed of any health risks Quebec may have. It is now more crucial than ever to be aware of the travel warnings and security precautions in effect for the location you are traveling to due to the COVID-19 epidemic. Do your homework on the most recent public health recommendations for preventing COVID-19 in Quebec, including wearing masks in public places, keeping a distance from people, and adhering to quarantine procedures before traveling there.

Visitors to Quebec in the winter may face health risks due to the cold weather. Pack warm gear to keep comfortable and reduce your risk of hypothermia or frostbite.

A translator app or a little card with a translation of their ailment and any drugs they are taking should always be carried by travelers with medical issues. Due to the dual language use in Quebec, it is crucial to have information accessible in both French and English.

Exploring Natural Wonders In Safety

The breathtaking landscapes of Quebec, including the Laurentian Mountains and the animals of the Boreal Forest, draw outdoor enthusiasts from all over the world. Take the necessary safety procedures while visiting these natural marvels to reduce risks:

1. Whether hiking, skiing, or biking, having a clear plan and discussing it with someone before setting off on your excursion is critical. Plan your route and let someone know your itinerary.

2. Carry the necessities: Pack a first aid kit, bug repellent, a map, a compass, and a whistle. Be mindful of the weather and dress accordingly.

3. To explore Quebec outdoors, consider hiring a local tour. A professional guide may improve your trip while ensuring your safety.

With its alluring fusion of natural beauty, culture, and history, Quebec is a safe tourist destination that never fails to win over tourists. Although the province is typically safe, exercising care and adopting simple safety measures is essential to guarantee a relaxing and worry-free trip. For a memorable trip to Quebec, keep up with the most recent travel warnings, adhere to recommended health and safety precautions, and respect local customs and traditions.

SAFETY SUGGESTIONS FOR QUEBEC

Travelers from all over the globe want to visit Quebec because of its storied past, fascinating culture, and beautiful scenery. Although the province is usually seen to be secure for visitors, it's crucial to remember a few safety precautions to enjoy your vacation the most. This guide will discuss being safe throughout your trip to Quebec.

Be mindful of your surroundings: Just as in every other place you visit, Quebec requires that you be mindful of your surroundings. Even though the neighborhood is regarded as secure, visitors should exercise caution in large places like festivals and stay away from strange places and late-night solo walks. Watch your valuables, particularly in busy or tourist areas, to prevent pickpocketing.

Wildlife is abundant in Quebec, including moose and black bears, so take care of them. Always be cautious, keep your distance from wildlife in national parks or rural regions, and never approach or feed the animals. To guarantee your safety, educate yourself on appropriate conduct near animals and what to do in case of an encounter.

Respect regional traditions and cultural norms: Quebec is noted for its bilingualism, with French and English is widely spoken, particularly in its main cities. Try to learn a few fundamental

French words to prevent misunderstandings and respect the natives. If your language abilities aren't flawless, don't panic; many people in Quebec know English and are willing to assist.

Pick your lodgings wisely by extensively researching the property and the area before making a reservation. Check the status of necessary facilities and read feedback left by past visitors. Choose lodgings close to public transit in a well-lit, busy neighborhood to increase convenience and safety.

Be ready for the weather since it may change drastically throughout the year in Quebec, from harsh winters to hot summers. Before your journey, check the weather forecast and prepare appropriately, including clothes for possible harsh circumstances. When engaging in outdoor activities like hiking or skiing, prepare for any weather-related situations by packing the right gear and telling someone about your intentions.

Observe traffic regulations: If you want to hire a vehicle or bicycle in Quebec, educate yourself on the region's traffic regulations and road signs. Give yourself plenty of time to respond if you see any animals crossing the road, particularly if you live in a rural region. Consider utilizing snow tires or chains and be ready for slippery situations if you must drive during the winter.

Be courteous in public areas: Follow instructions and appreciate the location's cultural and historical value while visiting tourist attractions or historic sites. Avoid rude actions like garbage, loud noises, and graffiti. By being respectful, you improve the experience for you and other guests while ensuring your safety.

Assistance and hospitality: The people of Quebec are renowned for their friendliness and hospitality. Never be afraid to seek help from neighbors or the police if you need it or feel frightened. Nine hundred eleven should be called in emergency cases across Canada, including Quebec.

You'll be ready for a pleasant vacation to Quebec if you keep these safety recommendations in mind. You'll surely have a terrific and safe time touring this beautiful Canadian province if you watch for your surroundings, follow local customs, and have a spirit of adventure.

Is Quebec secure at night?

The biggest province in Canada, Quebec, is renowned for its thriving culture, beautiful scenery, and old-world buildings. Quebec's low crime rate and welcoming culture, one of the safest cities in the world, make it a popular tourism destination. Some measures must be taken to protect your safety, just as anywhere you go. The safety of Quebec at night will be covered in this book, along with helpful advice on how to make the most of your nighttime explorations.

Keeping safe at night in Quebec:

Even at night, visitors and residents alike are said to feel secure in Quebec. According to a recent survey, Quebec is one of the top ten safest cities in North America. However, it is crucial to use caution while traveling around the city after dark, just as you would anywhere else.

Avoid these areas:

Although Quebec is usually safe, there are a few particular areas where you should exercise caution. For instance, despite major redevelopment, there may still be pockets of crime in the Saint-Roch area. The secluded location of certain areas of the city's Lower Town may also make them less secure. It is crucial to study your locations in advance and be aware of any safety advice.

Getting Around at Night:

Even late at night, using Quebec's public transit is dependable and secure. Taxis and buses are both great ways to get about. If ride-sharing services like Uber are more your style, they are available all across Quebec City. When utilizing any mode of transportation, pay attention to your possessions, keep your phone or other valuables out of sight, and choose well-lit, busy places to wait for your journey.

Eveninglife Security:

Quebec City has a vibrant nighttime scene with many activities, from clubs and pubs to festivals and numerous cultural events. Despite the fact that these places are normally secure, you must take precautions to protect yourself. Always stick with your buddies or tour group; avoid wandering alone in strange places.

Be careful while drinking alcohol, and never leave your beverages unattended. Respect local rules and ordinances governing smoking and alcohol usage.

Safety Advice for Nighttime Exploration in Quebec

1. Avoid going out alone at night; instead, travel in groups. The likelihood of encountering a dangerous circumstance decreases with the number of individuals you are with.

2. Keep your possessions safe by being aware of them and refraining from flashing precious jewelry when out at night.

3. Use your intuition: If anything seems odd, go with your gut and leave the situation right away.

4. Learn the local emergency numbers so you can immediately call the police, an ambulance, or other emergency services in an emergency.

5. Dress correctly to avoid drawing unwanted attention. Be modest and discreet in your attire.

6. Be mindful of your surroundings and avoid using headphones or being too preoccupied with your phone, which might make you a target.

7. Keep to populated, well-lit locations: Remain in areas with many people and good illumination.

Although Quebec is known for its safety, it is still important to use common sense and take safety measures to protect yourself. You are well on your way to having a pleasurable, safe, and gratifying time in this interesting city by paying attention to the advice in this book.

Is it safe for a woman to visit Quebec alone?

Whether a traveler is planning a solo adventure in vibrant Montreal or a tranquil vacation in stunning Quebec City, safety should always come first. Quebec, often known as La Belle Province or the Beautiful Province, is considered a safe and welcoming location for single female tourists. Given its extensive history, diverse culture, and magnificent natural beauty, it is not surprising that visitors from all over the world visit this charming province of Canada.

We'll go over safety in Quebec in more depth and discuss what you can do as a girl traveling alone to have a safe and enjoyable vacation if you're wondering, "Is Quebec safe for me?

Accept The Culture And Traditions.

Quebec is unique from the rest of Canada due to its particular culture and language, which most of its inhabitants speak. A happy and safe trip depends on respecting and accepting local traditions and customs. Your journey will be more enjoyable and safe if you tolerate the Quebecois way of life, whether respecting the importance of their official language, French, or partaking in their many festivals and celebrations.

Taking Public Transportation and Walking

The public transportation systems in Quebec are reliable, efficient, and secure. Solitary female travelers may comfortably utilize the Métro, buses, and RTC bus network in Montreal and Quebec City since these modes of transportation are secure. Keep your belongings close by and pay attention to your surroundings while using public transportation.

It's normally safe to wander during the day, particularly in populated locations like Montreal and Quebec City. However, use caution while out and about at night, especially in uncharted territory. Be aware of your surroundings, stick to well-lit streets, steer clear of deserted parks and alleys, and always follow your gut.

Select Secure Lodging

Conduct extensive research on lodging options to protect your safety when visiting Quebec. By providing female-only floors and rooms, a lot of hostels, hotels, and Airbnb alternatives cater particularly to female tourists traveling alone. Reserve a room at a well-kept, well-regarded hotel in a prominent, secure area.

Connect With Locals And Other Travelers

Connecting with other tourists and locals is one of the many benefits of traveling alone. The people of Quebec are renowned for being kind and welcoming, so everywhere you go, feel free to start a discussion and make new acquaintances. You may meet individuals who share your interests through apps like Couchsurfing, Meetup, or local Facebook groups. These services can also advise you on fun and safe things to do in Quebec.

Be Cautious With Your Possessions And Your Safety

As with any trip location, monitoring your personal safety and property is critical. Although pickpocketing and purse snatching occurrences are rare in Quebec, they may occur, especially in crowded places like congested public transit or prominent tourist destinations. When exploring, keep valuables concealed and only bring what is necessary.

Take The Necessary Security Measures

Lastly, whether you're a solitary female traveler, using basic prudence is critical. Ensure copies of important papers are available, including your passport, identification, and travel insurance. Give a reliable contact back home a copy of your itinerary and keep them informed of your location. Most importantly, always rely on your instincts regarding your security and well-being.

Quebec is a beautiful and secure place for female visitors traveling alone. You may securely tour this beautiful Canadian province's beauty and charm by adhering to the abovementioned rules and being aware of your safety.

QUEBEC SCAMS

Travelers love Quebec because of its picturesque cobblestone streets, breathtaking scenery, and delectable cuisine. Although it is generally considered a secure destination for vacations, you should be cautious of any possible scams you could run across. Our travel guide attempts to provide you with useful information to assist you in identifying and preventing scams while visiting Quebec.

ATM and Currency Scams

Keep an eye out for skimmers or modified ATMs while using them. These tools grab your card details so that fraudsters may subsequently utilize them. To reduce danger, always use ATMs in well-lit places, ideally inside hotels or banks. Use caution while utilizing card readers in restaurants and retail establishments. In order to get your data, thieves may sometimes replace the original card reader with a tampered one. If you see anything fishy, use cash instead or use a different terminal.

Fraudulent Booking and Accommodations

It is recommended to utilize trustworthy and well-established platforms, including well-known online booking services or travel agencies when making tours, performances, or lodging reservations. Although it could seem tempting, avoid buying tickets or making hotel reservations from random strangers on the street or via unreliable web advertising since they might be fake or costly. Before making any reservations, always check the website's validity and ask your hotel for advice.

Taxi Fraud

Even cab drivers may try to defraud visitors by taking longer routes or failing to use the meter, resulting in exorbitant prices. Use ride-hailing services like Uber to prevent this, or request transportation from your hotel. If you must take a taxi, be sure the driver uses the proper meter and knows your broad location knowledge. Get acquainted with the usual prices and have a map to prevent overcharging.

Embezzlement and theft

Quebec is typically secure like any other tourist site, yet it might be a target for opportunistic theft. Keep closely checking your possessions in a busy area, such as Old Quebec, a market, or a railway station. Use zipped pockets to store your wallet, phone, and camera; stay away from backpacks with open-access sections. Invest in a money belt or secret bag to protect your cash, passport, and other valuables.

False charity fraud

Be wary of someone claiming to be from a non-profit organization or working for a charity. Con artists often use this strategy to exploit travelers' compassion and collect money under false pretenses. If you want to donate to a local cause, research and choose a reliable group to support you.

fake friendship bracelets

In this scam, a kind stranger may approach you and try to tie a "friendship bracelet" around your wrist before demanding money. Although uncommon in Quebec, use caution if you encounter one. Politely decline and go as soon as you can.

Even though Quebec is a generally secure place to visit, you should always travel with caution and vigilance. Take reasonable measures, such as safeguarding your property, checking the credentials of tour providers and lodgings, and keeping an eye out for red flags in potentially dangerous circumstances. By doing this, you can make sure your vacation to Quebec is fun, memorable, and free of scams.

HOW TO RESPOND
IN AN EMERGENCY

I t's crucial to be ready for any emergency circumstance that can occur when traveling in the stunning province of Quebec. This book will provide useful advice on what to do and who to call in an emergency, ensuring you are prepared to face any unexpected situations. At the same time, you discover Quebec's sights and sounds.

Knowing Quebec's emergency phone number is a must before anything else for your protection. To contact police, fire, and medical services in an emergency, call 911. This number works all around Canada and is accessible all the time.

Being able to provide first responders with your location when handling situations precisely. Learn important geographic information, such as neighboring landmarks, street names, and local sites of interest, before starting your excursions in Quebec. Additionally, ensure you always have a well-charged GPS-enabled mobile phone.

It's important to periodically check the weather forecast while in Quebec, particularly if you plan to hike in a remote region or during the winter. Knowing the weather in advance allows you to make appropriate plans for situations when severe storms or very high temperatures might pose serious hazards.

Knowing the locations of the closest hospitals or clinics is crucial in the event of a medical emergency. Several healthcare facilities are accessible to address emergencies in large cities like Montreal and Quebec City. However, in certain isolated locations, access to medical treatment may only be available after some time. In these cases, be ready with a well-stocked first aid kit and consider getting travel insurance that covers emergency evacuation.

It's critical to respond when lost or stolen things, such as wallets or passports, are involved. Report the incident to the neighborhood police force. In addition, get in touch with your embassy or consulate for help replacing stolen or lost passports. Ensure you have photocopies or digital copies of important papers in a safe area as a preventative precaution.

Accidents on the road may occur everywhere, even in Quebec. In an automobile accident, keep your composure and put your safety first. If there is any possible threat, evaluate the situation and call 911 if necessary. With the other parties involved, trade contact and insurance details; if practical, take pictures of the situation.

Finally, in strange situations, always follow your instincts and behave cautiously. By adhering to these recommendations, you'll be well-equipped to manage any emergency issues while traveling, enabling you to concentrate on making priceless memories. At the same time, you explore the beautiful province of Quebec.

PROTECTION AGAINST TRAVEL RISKS

L et's talk travel protection insurance in depth to prepare you for a wonderful and hassle-free time as we go on our adventure to see Quebec's enthralling beauty. A well-planned journey begins with securing your vacation and providing peace of mind in knowing that you are protected should unforeseen circumstances happen, whether in Quebec City's stunning surroundings or Montreal's hectic city life.

The Importance of Travel Protection Insurance for Your Adventure in Quebec

Even if you may visualize the ideal vacation to Quebec, unexpected things might still happen. Travel protection insurance gives you the peace of mind to enjoy your trips without worrying about complications. The following are some advantages of purchasing travel insurance:

1. Nobody likes to experience travel-related catastrophes like cancellations, delays, or misplaced bags. These unforeseen events, however, may occur at any moment. You may reduce the financial pressures of travel-related setbacks by purchasing travel protection insurance, ensuring that your well-earned trip is pleasurable and stress-free.

2. Medical Emergencies: A successful trip requires good health. Travel insurance can provide you coverage for emergency medical

expenses if you or any of your traveling companions have a medical problem while in Quebec. This is true for accidents, injuries, and even sudden dental problems.

3. Theft and Loss: Whether strolling through Quebec City's picturesque streets or seeing Montreal's Notre Dame Basilica, you should look for possible theft and loss hazards. Travel insurance guarantees you will be paid for lost or stolen belongings, including gadgets, credit cards, and passports. Some insurance plans may aid with acquiring emergency funds if necessary.

Choosing The Proper Insurance For Your Trip

Choosing the ideal travel protection insurance is an important choice to make while organizing your Quebec journey. When comparing insurance coverage, consider the following:

1. Identify Your Needs: Your insurance should be tailored to your travel needs, considering details like the duration of your trip, the activities you want to participate in, and any current medical issues that could need more extensive coverage.

2. Read the terms and conditions: Each policy provides specifics such as coverage restrictions, policy exclusions, and claim filing guidelines. To prevent unpleasant surprises on your vacation, be aware of these things.

3. Compare prices and Benefits: A minimum of three providers should be considered when comparing the prices and advantages of various travel protection insurance policies to guarantee that you get the best deal possible. It's important to examine all the relevant criteria before selecting since even the most expensive travel insurance policy may only sometimes be the best option. Travel insurance policies only sometimes provide the most coverage, and neither do the cheapest ones.

Making Use Of Your Travel Protection Insurance While In Quebec

Prepare to use your travel protection insurance effectively if anything goes wrong during your excursion to Quebec. Here are some actions to take:

1. Contact Your Insurance Provider: Be sure to contact your insurance provider as soon as possible. They will walk you through your particular circumstance and advise you of your important actions.

2. File Claims Quickly: Most insurance companies demand that you submit your claims within a certain period, so be mindful of deadlines for medical expenses, time-sensitive situations, or lost property.

3. save All Paperwork: In the event of any issue you may encounter while you are in Quebec, be sure to save all pertinent documents, such as invoices, receipts, and evidence of expenditures. In order to efficiently process your claim, we will require this information. Remember that traveling to Quebec should be an amazing experience full of adventure and excitement, and purchasing travel protection insurance will provide you peace of mind while you're away. To ensure a pleasant and pleasurable trip in lovely Quebec, be ready, be safe, and take prompt action in the event of any unforeseen problems.

ACCOMMODATIONS IN QUEBEC

Finding the ideal lodging is crucial as you organize your amazing trip to Quebec if you want to take full advantage of this stunning Canadian province. After a day of visiting Quebec's rich culture and breathtaking natural beauty, this guide will give you an understanding of the wide choice of available accommodations.

Montreal: The Dynamic City

The biggest city in Quebec, Montreal, has a vibrant and energetic environment. If you want to enjoy Quebec's thriving arts and cultural scene, famous eating establishments, and nightlife, this buzzing city is a great spot to stay.

Consider staying in Old Montreal if you want to immerse yourself in the history of the area. The exquisite Hotel Nelligan and the opulent Hotel William Gray are just two of the lovely boutique hotels and bed & breakfasts that can be found in this historic area. These lodgings combine contemporary conveniences with the neighborhood's distinctive old-world charm.

However, Downtown Montreal is home to a large selection of top-notch hotels, like the Ritz-Carlton and the opulent Le Mount Stephen, if you prefer more modern settings. This location is a great option for tourists who want the convenience of being near attractions like the Museum of Fine Arts, the upmarket stores of

Rue Sainte-Catherine, or the cutting-edge Quartier des Spectacles.
Quebec City: A Touch of Europe in the Americas

The provincial capital of Quebec City is renowned for its breathtaking historical sites, charming ambiance, and undeniable European charm. The highlight of your trip to Quebec will undoubtedly be your stay in this charming location.

Consider booking accommodation in Old Quebec, a UNESCO World Heritage site, to experience the city's distinctive appeal fully. This walled city has several historic hotels, including the magnificent Fairmont Le Château Frontenac, which dominates the skyline. Auberge Saint-Antoine, a stunning boutique hotel in Lower Town that offers a tranquil setting and individualized service, is a fantastic choice.

Outside the borders of the city, you may discover areas like Saint-Roch, Saint-Jean-Baptiste, and Montcalm that provide a variety of chic hostels, inexpensive hotels, and inviting houses and breakfasts. These districts still have a laid-back vibe close to Quebec City's top sights.

Retreats in the Outdoors in Quebec

Here are some suggestions to whet your appetite for nature-filled experiences if you yearn for a peaceful setting among Quebec's magnificent surroundings.

Consider vacationing in one of the numerous ski resorts, such as Mont-Tremblant or Le Massif de Charlevoix, if you're an outdoor enthusiast looking for an enchanted winter paradise. These resorts have hospitable hotels and lodges that may be booked at different prices.

Explore the Eastern Townships nearby Montreal and provide a lakeside escape. This scenic area uniquely blends outdoor thrills, gastronomic delights, and rural charm. Stay at an opulent spa resort like Balnea or the charming Manoir Hovey, a magnificent Lake Massawippi shoreline inn.

Beautiful provincial parks and wildlife reserves in Quebec also provide uncommon lodging choices like comfortable chalets, eco-lodges, or camping grounds where you can take in the area's natural beauty while participating in various outdoor activities like hiking, canoeing, or animal viewing.

Quebec offers various lodging options suited to each traveler's requirements, preferences, and financial situation. If you're looking for an excellent urban stay, beautiful boutique hotels, historic districts, enchanted nature getaways, or affordable choices, Quebec's many landscapes provide what you want.

MATERIALS FOR TRAVEL

H aving the appropriate tools and trustworthy information is crucial when planning travel to Quebec to guarantee a smooth and enjoyable visit. You may discover a variety of information on many travel-related topics in this book to aid you in making the most of your vacation. Our Quebec travel guide covers everything, from lodging and transportation to attractions and safety.

Transport: Quebec has a variety of transportation options to fit a range of tastes and price ranges. Consider the following alternatives to tour the province efficiently:

1. Major airports include Mont Tremblant International, Quebec City-Jean Lesage, and Montreal-Trudeau. Domestic flights are served by several smaller airports, making it simple to reach the province's most rural regions.

2. Public transportation is the most accessible and cost-effective in big cities like Montreal and Quebec City. Both cities include substantial bus, rail, and metro networks, as well as daily, weekly, and monthly passes for visits of a longer duration.

3. Renting a vehicle allows you to explore Quebec's charming villages, interesting cities, and natural surroundings at your own pace. There are various facilities for major vehicle rental companies both at airports and around the province. Before

starting your road journey, make careful to research local traffic laws.

4. Taxis and ride-sharing services, such as Uber, are practical solutions for short trips inside cities. Remember that prices may increase during peak hours and on special occasions.

Accommodations: Quebec has a variety of lodging choices to suit a variety of preferences and price ranges.

1. Hotels: Quebec offers various lodging alternatives, from high-end hotels and boutique properties to affordable motels. Expedia, Booking.com, and Hotels.com are just a few great resources you can use to compare costs and locate the best deal.

2. Consider vacation homes from sites like Airbnb, VRBO, or HomeAway for longer stays and a more authentic experience. Travelers have a rare chance with these lodgings to stay in residential areas and taste local life.

Attractions: Quebec has a dynamic urban culture, breathtaking natural scenery, and a rich cultural legacy. Some attractions that are a must-see include:

1. Old Quebec: A lovely and historic area of Quebec City, Old Quebec is a UNESCO World Heritage Site. A lovely journey through history is made possible by cobblestone lanes, brightly painted homes, and historical buildings.

2. Montreal: As the province's main city, Montreal has top-notch food, shopping, and festivals. A unique blend of old-world beauty and contemporary city life should be noticed.

3. Mont-Tremblant is a well-liked location for skiing, hiking, and town exploring since it offers year-round outdoor activities.

4. The Gaspe Peninsula is a must-see for nature enthusiasts because of its stunning coastline scenery, amazing fauna, and lovely fishing communities.

Safety: In general, traveling to Quebec is secure, but taking the required security measures is always a good idea.

1. Emergency Services: To contact police, fire, or medical assistance in an emergency, phone 911. Carry your cell phone with you and ensure it is compatible with the regional network.

2. Travel Insurance: Getting travel insurance is advised to guard

against unplanned costs associated with sickness, accident, or theft.

3. Quebec is a province that speaks mostly French, although English is also extensively used. Learn some actual French words and phrases, and for convenience, take a pocket dictionary or a translation app.

4. Weather: Depending on the season, Quebec has a variety of weather conditions. Be cautious to prepare sensibly and monitor local predictions during your visit.

TOP 10 HOTELS IN QUEBEC FOR LUXURY

Y ou may search for the ideal lodging as you prepare for your Quebec trip. Quebec is renowned for its extensive history and culture and its range of opulent hotels. Here is a list of the top 10 opulent hotels in Quebec that provide elegance, charm, and first-rate service to assist you in making your choice.

The Fairmont chain's Le Château Frontenac, a famous castle-like hotel with regal grandeur and unrivaled views of the St. Lawrence River, is in the center of Old Quebec. In addition to having three excellent restaurants, a spa, and a fitness facility, the hotel also has tastefully appointed guest rooms and suites.

The Auberge Saint-Antoine is a modern boutique hotel constructed on a notable archaeological site located in Quebec City's historic Old Port neighborhood. The hotel's decor deftly combines contemporary and antiquity, and each room has special treasures and great facilities for a customized stay. An acclaimed eating establishment is the on-site Panache restaurant.

Manoir Hovey is a charming five-star hotel tucked away on the shores of Lake Massawippi and was designed in the style of George Washington's Mount Vernon residence. You may enjoy a tranquil getaway away from the bustle of the city in one of the luxurious bedrooms or lakeside villas. The Le Hatley Restaurant on the site is famous for serving outstanding meals.

Le Mount Stephen is a luxurious boutique hotel in Montreal housed in Lord George Stephen's former home. This hotel successfully combines traditional and modern styles. The exquisite suites offer modern conveniences, and the on-site Bar George provides magnificent décor and a top-notch eating experience.

Ritz-Carlton Montréal: Since 1912, the opulent Ritz-Carlton Montréal has catered to affluent tourists. This five-star hotel provides first-rate individual service, tasteful lodging, and a well-regarded spa. Fine dining is available at the renowned Maison Boulud restaurant by world-famous chef Daniel Boulud.

Fairmont Le Manoir Richelieu: This magnificent inn in the gorgeous Charlevoix area features spectacular St. Lawrence River vistas and outstanding architecture. Luxurious lodging, indoor and outdoor pools, and a top-notch golf course are available to guests. In addition, the hotel has a casino and a number of food options.

Hôtel Birks Montréal: This elegant boutique hotel is housed in a historic structure in downtown Montreal and offers a sleek, modern aesthetic. Le Kitchen, a restaurant with European influences, and the Spa Hammam are also available at the hotel.

Downtown Montreal's Hôtel Le Crystal is a five-star luxury boutique hotel with breathtaking views of the city and Mount Royal. The suites provide contemporary architecture and beauty, as well as contemporary conveniences and roomy living spaces. A spa, a fine-dining restaurant called Siam, and a heated indoor saltwater pool are among the amenities.

The Sofitel Montréal Golden Mile is a contemporary luxury hotel with a hint of French charm in the center of downtown Montreal. The hotel's Renoir restaurant delivers excellent French cuisine, and the bedrooms and suites feature floor-to-ceiling windows. The best places in the city to see, such as Sainte-Catherine Street and the Museum of Fine Arts, are easily accessible from the hotel.

In Baie-Saint-Paul, the contemporary, environmentally friendly Le Germain Hotel Charlevoix has distinctive architecture and creative design. The St. Lawrence River may be seen from Le

Germain, which provides a wonderful stay for visitors. Visitors may splurge at the hotel's two eateries, Le Bercail and Les Labours, and unwind in the tranquil Spa du Verger or the outdoor thermal pool at Le Germain.

To sum up, Quebec provides a variety of opulent hotels for a premium trip experience. Each of these top hotels guarantees great service, comfort, and extravagance, from Le Château Frontenac's historical beauty to Le Mount Stephen's modern elegance. Your journey in Quebec is waiting!

QUEBEC'S TOP 10 ATTRACTIONS AND ACTIVITIES

I t's important to research the top sights and activities this Canadian province offers as you prepare for your vacation to Quebec. Quebec has something to offer everyone, with rich history, culture, and natural beauty. The top 10 things to see and see in Quebec are included in this detailed guide.

Explore Old Quebec, a UNESCO World Heritage Site, to kick off your trip to Quebec. Cobblestone streets, ancient structures, and a wide variety of shops and eateries offer you a flavor of Europe in North America thanks to the city's more than 400-year heritage. Wander the Quartier Petit-Champlain's winding alleyways, see the magnificent Château Frontenac, and stroll along the Dufferin Terrace to take the St. Lawrence River's perspective.

Discover the magnificent waterfall at Montmorency Falls Park, which is 30 meters higher than Niagara Falls. Reach the suspension bridge for a stunning view of the falls by using a cable car or hiking the paths. Visit the spectacular ice wall created by the smashing waves throughout the winter for an exceptional experience.

Visit Montreal's renowned Notre Dame Basilica, a stunning example of Gothic Revival architecture from the late 19th century.

The basilica is more than simply a place of prayer because of its stunning stained glass windows and fascinating light displays. There are guided tours available, and if you go during an Aura light display, you'll be amazed by the inside of the church's illuminations.

Discover Parc National de la Jacques-Cartier, which provides a variety of outdoor activities, including hiking, canoeing, and fishing in a lovely, glacial valley surrounded by dense woods, to take in the natural beauty of the region. It's a great place to see the stunning hues of the changing leaves in the autumn.

To see the beautiful vistas of Quebec City and Lévis from the river, board the Quebec Ferry. The 15-minute journey provides a breathtaking vantage point from which to see the majesty and beauty of the area. Make sure your camera is prepared for some beautiful pictures.

Indulge in Canadian cuisine at one of the numerous sugar shacks in Quebec. Learn about the manufacture of maple syrup while enjoying a traditional supper that includes foods enhanced with maple flavor. On your tour, you should visit Le Chalet des Érables and Érablière Charbonneau, two well-liked sugar shacks.

Visit the Montreal Botanical Garden for a tranquil escape from the busy metropolis. Explore the 190 acres of beautiful gardens, greenhouses, and display areas that showcase plants from around the globe. Highlights include the serene Alpine Garden, the Chinese and Japanese Gardens, and the Insectarium.

Visit the Plains of Abraham, a key battleground that was crucial to Canada's history, and immerse yourself in the past. Learn about the events leading up to the 1759 fight and see the exhibition exhibiting relics from the site's archaeology by visiting the local museum.

Spend a day on the lovely island of Île d'Orléans, renowned for its illustrious agricultural history and delectable regional cuisine. Circulate the island by car or bicycle, stopping at quaint towns to take in the spectacular vistas and sample local food like wine, cheese, and chocolate.

Finally, visit Montreal's Museum of Fine Arts (Musée des Beaux-

Arts) to witness Quebec's distinctive fusion of art and culture. The museum has a sizable collection of works by well-known worldwide and Canadian painters, including Rembrandt, Picasso, and Monet. The Museum of Fine Arts in Quebec is a must-see attraction because of its on-site sculpture garden and several temporary exhibits.

Discovering these must-see locations and engaging in Quebec's unusual activities will undoubtedly help you generate lifelong memories that will compel you to visit this alluring province often.

TOP 10 DELECTABLE DISHES YOU SHOULD TRY

The wide variety of mouthwatering food waiting for you to discover will undoubtedly make your vacation memorable as you travel across the lovely province of Quebec. Quebec provides distinctive and delectable cuisine with distinct French and Canadian characteristics that must be noticed. Prepare your taste buds as we explore the top 10 delectable meals to sample while exploring Quebec.

The first item on our list is poutine, possibly Quebec's most well-known cuisine. Poutine consists of cheese curds on top of crisp fries covered in a delicious, thick sauce. From visitors to native Quebecers, everyone loves this comfort dish. Poutine may be found all around the province, but if you want to enjoy it, go for the locals' preferred location.

The classic dish tourtière, often offered during the winter holidays, must be tried next. This meat pie, native to the Lac-Saint-Jean region, often includes a ground pig, beef, or veal mixed with fragrant spices and covered in a flaky, buttery pastry crust. In restaurants and small bakeries all around Quebec, you may find tourtière.

Fish and seafood chowder is a traditional recipe that showcases

Quebec's wonderful seafood. Some could claim that Canada's other provinces can only partially match Quebec's great seafood selections. This chowder will quickly become a favorite once you take the first taste since it is thick, creamy, and packed with substantial pieces of fish, shrimp, and clams.

One must indulge in a Montreal-style bagel before leaving Quebec. These bagels have a unique texture and taste because they are hand-rolled, boiled in honey water, and baked in a wood-fired oven. Montreal bagels are superior to their New York counterparts because they are smaller, sweeter, and denser.

Try the renowned tarte au sucre, often known as sugar pie, if you have a sweet craving. This classic dish has a flaky pie crust encasing a creamy, velvety filling of milk and brown sugar. You'll want more because the crunchy, light crust and the sweet, silky filling have the ideal harmony of tastes and sensations.

Oka cheese, a semi-soft and creamy cheese with a subtle nutty taste, will delight cheese enthusiasts in Quebec. Oka cheese, developed by French Trappist monks, is a delightful complement to cheese boards or maybe savored with a hearty glass of wine.

The "Christ's ears" or "oreilles de crisse" are another distinctive Quebec specialty. Don't be offended by the name; these deep-fried, crispy pig rinds are a real treat. Ottes de crisse, which are salty and crispy, go well with a cold Quebec beer.

Sandwiches with smoked meat are a must-try while eating in Quebec. Montreal smoked meat is a special treat sometimes likened to pastrami or corned beef. Smoked meat sandwiches, which are tender, savory, and served on rye bread with mustard, will have you return for more.

Another typical Quebecois dish is creations, a spread prepared from ground pork, onions, and seasonings. This delicious spread is a standard at traditional Québécois breakfast settings and is often served on fresh crusty bread or toast. It could end up being a standard on yours as well!

Finally, treat yourself to genuine maple syrup products widely available in Quebec. Enjoy sweets like maple taffy, created by drizzling hot maple syrup over just-fallen snow, and maple sugar candies during the annual "Sugar Shack" season. There's a reason why Quebec's maple syrup is so well-known; once you try it, there's no turning back!

Along with satisfying your palate, this culinary tour of Quebec will deepen your understanding of the region's rich history and legacy. While you discover these top 10 delectable Quebecois cuisine, remember to cherish each mouthful.

CONCLUSION

Your trip to Quebec will be amazingly packed with stunning natural scenery, a vibrant culture, and delectable culinary treats. You will be enthralled by this region's unique appeal and the kind welcome of its inhabitants as you travel through it. The relationships and experiences you make will be treasured mementos of the many adventures you had in this fascinating region.

Consider how much of the broad and diverse offers of the province you were able to experience as you look back on your trip to Quebec. Each visit provides an unprecedented insight into the many facets of Quebecois culture, whether in the vibrant, international city of Montreal or the medieval, cobblestone streets of Quebec City. Visitors will certainly get a positive impression of the province because of its seamless fusion of contemporary and historical.

Quebec's natural splendor is just as captivating, with its luxuriant woods, many freshwater lakes, stunning mountain ranges, and gorgeous provincial parks. The outdoors in Quebec proved to be the ideal escape from the stresses of contemporary life, whether you opted to kayak along the Saguenay Fjord, climb through the majestic Laurentian Mountains, or camp out beneath the stars in one of the province's gorgeous parks.

Your palate will also remind you of the abundant delectable foods in this special area. The province's diverse culinary landscape, which includes locally produced foods like tourtiere and poutine and international cuisine, reflects the region's rich legacy and its people's willingness to embrace new ideas. You were relishing in Quebec's rich cultural past and contemporary vitality as you relished its specialties, possibly at a quaint cafe, a trendy café, or a chic restaurant.

Last, we must pay attention to Quebec's real gems: its hospitable people. Every interaction is infused with real warmth and sincerity because of their contagious joie de vivre and loves for their country, language, and customs. You unquestionably felt engulfed by the colorful tapestry of Quebecoise life and ready to return for another visit because of their positive outlook.

Your trip to Quebec explored a fascinating, colorful, charming province that simultaneously seized your heart and imagination. Allow this guide to inspire future journeys to this beautiful location that will further strengthen your bond with a place that can now be considered unforgettable. As you continue to cherish the memories of the experiences you had and the relationships you made, do so.